MY OWN WORST ENEMY

how to stop holding yourself back

JANET DAVIS

BETHANYHOUSE
a division of Baker Publishing Group
Minneapolis, Minnesota

© 2012 by Janet Davis

Published by Bethany House Publishers
11400 Hampshire Avenue South
Bloomington, Minnesota 55438
www.bethanyhouse.com

Bethany House Publishers is a division of
Baker Publishing Group, Grand Rapids, Michigan

Printed in the United States of America

Library of Congress Cataloging-in-Publication Data

Davis, Janet,
    My own worst enemy : how to stop holding yourself back / Janet Davis.
      p. cm.
    Summary: "A retreat leader and speaker teaches women to recognize and overcome self-defeating behavior and begin living out their purpose in God's kingdom. Includes study questions for small groups"—Provided by publisher.
Includes bibliographical references.
    ISBN 978-0-7642-0950-5 (pbk. : alk. paper)
    1. Christian women—Religious life. 2. Self-actualization (Psychology) in women. 3. Self-actualization (Psychology)—Religious aspects—Christianity. I. Title.
BV4527.D375 2012
248.8′43—dc23   2011044569

The stories of women in this book are true. Some names and specific details have been altered to honor privacy.

This book is based on the experience of the author. It is not intended to take the place of professional or pastoral counseling.

The Internet addresses, email addresses, and phone numbers in this book are accurate at the time of publication. They are provided as a resource. Baker Publishing Group does not endorse them or vouch for their content or permanence.

Cover design by Connie Gabbert

12 13 14 15 16 17 18   7 6 5 4 3 2 1

This work is dedicated to the women in my world who have dared to shine, showing me the way forward.

Almighty God, you proclaim your truth in every age by many voices: Direct, in our time, we pray, those who speak where many listen and write what many read; that they may do their part in making the heart of this people wise, its mind sound, and its will righteous; to the honor of Jesus Christ our Lord. Amen.

The Book of Common Prayer

MY OWN
WORST
ENEMY

Contents

Contents

Foreword

Janet Davis came into my life unexpectedly. A listener to *Midday Connection*, the radio program I host, sent me one of her books and recommended I interview her. It's one thing to get a free book from a publisher, something that happens daily in my line of work. It's quite another for a person to invest money and time in buying a book, writing a letter, then paying to send it in hopes that the person on the other end listens to their request. I took this all into consideration when Janet's book arrived along with the heartfelt letter that accompanied it. At that point, I had no idea how much Janet would rock my world. As I dug into her writing, I knew she would become a regular guest on the program.

Eventually I invited her to a staff retreat for my small team, and we have never been the same. The retreat happened on Labor Day weekend a few years ago, and we still talk about pre–Labor Day and post–Labor Day thinking.

Janet's writing challenges the reader as well as affirms, all while posing thought-provoking questions that linger in the mind. Janet has the audacity to tell me, and all of us, through this book, *My Own Worst Enemy*, that I can SHINE, that I am called to shine. Since meeting Janet I've had the courage to write a book and edit two others, to speak up in my workplace and church, and to believe, really believe, that my feminine soul—along with what I bring to the table, wherever I am—truly matters!

What woman has not struggled with self-sabotage or hiding in the process of wanting to make a difference? Our very nature often puts us in a nurturing role where we take a backseat to others and end up believing that the backseat is the only seat we may occupy. Janet has a heart for calling women forward into the fullness of who God created us to be. If you have the courage to read on, and I hope you will, you'll become uncomfortable at times as well as encouraged. You will be called to imagine what a life well lived might look like. And as you begin to share your story of transformation, you'll have the opportunity to reach out beyond yourself and bring other women along with you.

Janet points us to the power of Christ within us. And when we tap into that power, we will see courage rise. She says that God invites us to partner with him and to be a shining presence. Sometimes, in order to get there, we need a wise mentor to come alongside us. Janet Davis is that wise mentor. She gives us language for what is happening in our interior world and helps expose what keeps us from caring for our souls. In the process, Janet authentically shares her own story. She tells about her own seasons of self-sabotage.

As we see our common struggle, as we hear those internal shaming voices, Janet reminds us of the command found in Matthew 5:16: "Let your light shine before others, that they may see your good deeds and glorify your Father in heaven." Go SHINE!

Anita Lustrea
Executive Producer and Host of Midday Connection
Author and speaker

Acknowledgments

To my husband, Bob, who welcomes my voice, fosters my growth, and encourages my work.

To our children, Bobby, Jenna, Joel, and Betsy, who ground my life, keep me honest, and broaden my vision.

To the women poets whose work has inspired me, many of whom have generously given me permission to include pieces of their work here.

Thanks to Janay and Melanie: my writing companions. Your friendship was an essential ingredient in this process.

Also thanks to my reading team: Christy, Cathy, Katy, Nancy, Missy, Mary, and Melinda, as well as Tracie, my manuscript formatting expert.

Thanks to the Midday team: Anita, Melinda, and Lori. Your encouragement, both in word and deed, has kept me focused on the importance of this work.

Thanks to my book club friends: Mary and Trisha. You have been my wise midwives in the pregnancy, labor, and delivery of this "child."

Thanks also to my spiritual directors consultation group. You have held me with tender compassion as I have sought to allow this message to come alive in me.

Thanks to Andy, a wise man, and the staff of Bethany House, who were willing to listen to and trust the voices of women as they advocated for the healing message of this book to become more broadly available. Thanks also to Ellen, my wise and sensitive editor, who worked hard to make this healing message accessible to more women.

And finally, to the women who have allowed me to tell their stories in this book. Your faith, beauty, and courage inspire me.

Introduction

This Little Light of Mine

The glory of God is [wo]man, fully alive.[1]

SAINT IRENAEUS

A Curiosity Born: I have met the enemy

"I have an offer I'd like you to consider." My theology professor Ken and I were having coffee together at a Seattle's Best near our school in Kirkland, Washington. We'd been discussing the book of Ruth, an ancient story that had recently captivated me, when he made me an offer I couldn't refuse.

"You see things in that story of women that I can't see," he said, "the internal dynamics, the relational aspects. We will be doing an overview of Ruth in a few weeks in the Old Testament Survey course you are in. Would you consider teaching a part of the class? You could have as much time as you'd like. I really think you have a lot to offer."

Though I wasn't sure it was okay to admit it to myself, or out loud, there was a part of me that knew he was right: As insightful and well-educated as my professor was, I did see things he had not. I did have a lot to offer. That confident part of me said, "Sure, I'd love to."

There was also a part of me that was not so self-assured. Fairly comfortable with public speaking, I spent a lot of time gathering my thoughts, motivated both by my passion for the subject at hand and a lingering insecurity. I planned exercises and engaging questions. I worked and practiced and was genuinely excited for this opportunity to speak to my peers about what I saw in the book of Ruth. I had a lot to say and a genuine sense that it would be helpful to others in the class. All in all, I had about forty-five minutes worth of content.

The day arrived. The classroom was bright, but far from warm in the damp chill of a Pacific Northwest February. The two walls of windows let in abundant, gently buffered light from the cloudy Seattle skies. The institutional linoleum, looming chalkboards, and laminate-topped student desks, however, negated any sense of warmth the light provided. Gathered in a room designed for a larger group, a tinny sound bounced from all those hard surfaces as we settled into our seats.

The pre-class banter was friendly and hospitable. By this point in the semester, I knew all my twenty or so classmates pretty well. In our small graduate school program, we had many classes together, including counseling practicum, allowing us to become acquainted from the inside out. There was quite an age and gender mix in this particular class, ranging from the twenties to the sixties. It was a comfortable crowd.

About twenty minutes into our three-hour-lecture class, Ken gave me the floor. Though he removed his notes from the lectern, offering it to me, I simply stood where I was, in the middle of the room, said a few sentences, and sat down.

Finished. I presented only a fraction of my material. I offered it very casually, as if off-the-cuff and unintentional. I had refused the podium. I did whatever I could in that moment to diminish my voice and contribution.

So, you might ask, what happened? I was asking the same question—not only that day but for months to come. What caused me to sabotage this lovely and sincere invitation to speak my insights and wisdom? Why was I afraid to shine? The faces were welcoming, and the opportunity for doing something good was real. So what unseen force had shifted me into reverse? Clearly, the problem was internal. I had met the enemy and she was *me.*

An Accusing Script Uncovered: the words beneath the choice

As I began to explore that moment, I first examined my internal experience. Though there was much life and creativity within me around the topic at hand, when I rose to speak, it was as if a heavy wet blanket began to shroud my whole being, dousing my internal light. I wanted to disappear or crawl under my desk. Listening internally to my voice, all I heard was a monotone muffled murmur. All of the emotion and enthusiasm that had inspired Ken's invitation had vanished. My mind became a dense, soupy fog. I spoke mechanically and vacantly, as the living dead. The only thing I could discern clearly, just beneath the surface, was an unspoken yet resounding question: "Just who do you think you are?"

Just who do you think you are? The contemptuous tone attached to those words made them more of a belittling accusation than a question. The answer was *You are nobody, and you have nothing of value to say.* I knew intuitively that somewhere within those words was the key to the strong undertow that sucked my voice into silence.

A Journey of Observations: a common struggle

That painful speaking experience began a journey of focused and unfolding observation for me. At first it centered on those seven words: *Just who do you think you are?* They echoed inside me more often than I wanted to admit. I could clearly see that they had become a significant hindrance to shining, to living out the fullness of who God had created me to be. I wondered if the same thing was true for other women.

As I accepted the personal challenge of dealing with these powerfully silencing words, I also began asking other women about their own experiences of self-sabotage. Most could readily recall a story in which their beauty, goodness, or voice was censored by that shaming mantra. I was amazed by how many actually used those precise words as they told their stories of self-defeat. Some had labeled their behavior as self-sabotage, some had not. Some episodes were obvious, some more subtle. All suspected that a God-sourced light within had been doused or hidden. *Ugh.* Many struggled to figure out what part pride had to play in their internal shutdown response, often abandoning that struggle without further insight. Let me offer a few highlights.

One of the first women I spoke with was a recent graduate from the master's program I was attending. She was job hunting and really struggling: "Every time I read the list of qualification requirements or job description, I'd think, *Just who do you think you are applying for that position? You don't know enough or have the kind of experience they want. Don't get in over your head!"* She continued, "I am so frustrated with myself. I know that's true for some of the jobs, but not all of them. And I hear that every time. In fact, dealing with that internal script is by far the hardest part of this job search."

Another woman talked about battling self-sabotage as she was waiting for votes to be counted in a church leadership election. "You know, I came so close to taking my name off the ballot." She was elected by an overwhelming majority and almost missed this opportunity to shine in service to her obviously supportive community. A third woman was grieving the end of her third marriage. All three men were alcoholics. Both her sad eyes and slumped shoulders seemed to scream, "Why do I keep doing this to myself?"

Two things to note in each self-sabotage tale: First, the women spoke with a sense of surprise at the harsh and seemingly believable tone of their own internal dialogue. Second, they shared a deep sense of painful helplessness—almost despair—from their lack of understanding about this enemy within. The more I observed, the more I saw self-sabotage as a widespread problem. I became acutely aware of how many awesome and gifted women spent significant amounts of time and energy neglecting, dismissing, or actively covering up their beauty and talent. Not to mention how many God-inspired, creative voices and ventures had been stolen outright, aborted, or prematurely shut down by this powerful force.

Shining Is Not Pride

It is not surprising that some of the women I spoke with were more than a little uncomfortable talking about this topic of self-sabotage, especially when my assumption was that shining would be the healthier alternative. Good Christian women have been taught for generations that it is rude to talk about oneself, much less to shine. It seems that there is a great deal of confusion in our Christian culture about pride and shining as well as hiding and humility.

"This little light of mine, I'm gonna let it shine." That little song is not idle chatter; it is based on Scripture.

> *You are the light of the world. A town built on a hill cannot be hidden. Neither do people light a lamp and put it under a bowl. Instead they put it on its stand, and it gives light to everyone in the house. In the same way, let your light shine before others, that they may see your good deeds and glorify your Father in heaven. (Matthew 5:14–16)*

The verse makes plain the reality that shining is not just a nice option; it is our calling.

The Bible shares the stories of particular people who shine in particular ways, like Moses (Exodus 34:29–35) and John the Baptist (John 5:35), prophets who have insight (Daniel 12:3), the righteous in the parable of the wheat and the tares (Matthew 13:43), and Jesus' radiant bride, the church (Ephesians 5:27). There are many other places where the idea of shining is referenced (Proverbs 13:9; Philippians 2:15–17; Psalm 34:5; Luke 11:33–36; 2 Corinthians 4:6).

Think about it: Would God call us to shine if shining were inherently prideful? Of course not! Though a healthy aversion to pride is a good thing, *shining is not pride*. And therefore, avoidance of pride is not an acceptable explanation for our refusal to shine. Confused? Perhaps the other side of this coin is easier to see.

Hiding Is Not Humility

"Hide it under a bushel? *No!*" Hiding is not humility. When we confuse pride and shining, we also often confuse hiding and humility. Though initially a tempting thought and a commonly used excuse, it is shortsighted to believe that we can best deal with one sin (pride) by engaging in another (hiding), or refusing to shine.

Think about a woman who does an incredible job of directing a women's retreat. Grateful participants come to her: "This was amazing. You are so good at this kind of thing. Thank you so much." The typical reply: "Oh, really, it wasn't me. God did this in spite of me; anything good you see is all God." She makes herself out to be a zero, invisible, a negative number in a moment when she and God have clearly worked something beautiful together. Think for a moment about the difference in this reply: "Thank you so much." *Pause.* "It has been fun getting to do something in line with my gifts. I am amazed at what God does in and through and around us! The most enjoyable part was matching various jobs to the gifts and passions of the women. We all got to shine!"

The root of the word *humble* comes from the idea of "ground" or "earth." To be humble is to be aware of our human nature, its earthy physicality, dignity, and limitations. It is definitely *not* to be invisible, a zero, or a negative number in the equation. Paul calls us to think rightly and soberly about ourselves (Romans 12:3–8). And he follows that admonition up with a list of our gifts, instructing us to use them to their fullest and with passion. We are gifted and unique. We are limited and frail. We have gifts to offer others: gifts others need. Hiding only hinders our ability to see and celebrate the glory of God at work in community.

Of course God is at work in us. *Of course* we would falter without him. At the same time, it is a fallacy to believe that in acknowledging our human contributions and even our imparted glory as a critically important part of God's divine work on earth, we are being prideful. God's glory is not dimmed one iota by our full and shining presence. God has *invited* us to partner with him. How dare we regard the shining made-in-the-image-of-God person God has called us to be as a *nobody*. Remember this: Shining is not pride and hiding is not humility.

A Storied Conversation

Though there are many valid approaches to a discussion about self-sabotage, my personal preference as a spiritual director is to offer a storied conversation. Granted, there is no such thing as a typical story of self-sabotage; no two instances are ever the same. We are as unique in our hiding as we are in our shining. Our struggles layer personality over gender over culture over circumstance over relational styles over giftedness over harmful experiences over maturity, and on and on it goes.

Yet there are common internal experiences from the stories of others that resonate and help us put language to what's going on inside our own souls. Stories can expose our games and enlighten us even without offering us comprehensive or analytical understanding. They can inspire us and offer glimpses of a different path that can help us craft concrete plans for new freedom, real change, and bright shining. We can begin to imagine doing life differently, and hope can be born as stories are exchanged.

Just as important, shared stories may also help us feel less alone in this important struggle. The dynamic of being our own worst enemies carries with it an inherent self-containment and great temptation for isolation. Because so many of these dynamics operate below the waterline, they are rarely brought to awareness and even more rarely to conversation. We may feel ashamed and alone in what we sometimes see as our "personal craziness." But we are not alone. The more we talk about the ways self-sabotage hinders our radiance, the less power it has in our lives.

This is a book of gathered stories; in each chapter you will hear a modern and an ancient story that illustrates a particular aspect of our struggle with self-sabotage. At the end of each chapter, through thought-provoking questions, you will be invited to bring your own story into the conversation. I have loosely collected the stories into three sections.

Section 1, **Many Faces**, speaks of stories gathered around three different subtly self-sabotaging patterns of living: the unimagined life, the unworthy life, and the unlived life. Section 2, **Many Phases**, highlights different seasons in my own struggle. Section 3, **Choices Along the Way**, highlights healthy and proactive choices that can offer us more freedom from the destructive web in which we find ourselves.

To What End

Jesus, translating the prophets, described the good news:

> *The Spirit of the Lord is on me,*
> *because he has anointed me*
> *to proclaim good news to the poor.*

21

He has sent me to proclaim freedom for the prisoners
and recovery of sight for the blind,
to set the oppressed free,
to proclaim the year of the Lord's favor.
(Luke 4:18–19)

Freedom from poverty, bondage, oppression, and blindness: This is the good news work of God in the world both then and now. This is the nature of God's work in us as we move from self-sabotage to shining. May this be the fruit of both my labor and yours as we journey together through this book.

MANY FACES

1

The Unimagined Life

And now you must go out into your heart
as onto a vast plain. . . .[1]

RAINER MARIA RILKE

CONSIDER: Make a list of five subjects that you are so passionate about you would stay up late (or get up early) just to discuss them with friends.

Margaret

I spotted Margaret as I approached our gate at Houston Intercontinental Airport, just in time for boarding. After giving her a hug, I asked excitedly, "Did you bring your latest scrapbook? I can't wait to see it!"

"Oh no. Don't get me started here," Margaret said sadly. "I'll tell you all about it once we take off."

Margaret and I were heading to a women's retreat in California. We had lived around the corner from each other for several years as our children grew up in the same church and the same schools. Over the last seven years or so since my husband and I had moved away, we'd had some success at staying in touch.

Given Margaret's recent experience, I could understand the sadness. Her husband of twenty-plus years, Todd, had been diagnosed five years before with advanced cancer and died two years after his diagnosis. But scrapbooking was always a bright spot for her. I wondered what was up.

Once the plane was airborne, I leaned over and said, "Okay, spill it."

Margaret grinned and began quietly. "Well, I think it was last Tuesday. I was finishing up the scrapbook I told you about on the phone, the one for the twins' third birthday party. Surprisingly, as I put it up on the bookshelf, I felt this very strong and odd sense of emptiness. You would think I would have felt the opposite, right? Satisfaction, or something like that? But I didn't.

"After all these years of grieving for Todd, I knew not to ignore what I was feeling, no matter how crazy it felt. So I pulled out my journal and just started writing. And it was sadness, but it wasn't about Todd at all. It was about *me*."

"Okay," I said when she paused. "And . . ."

"I suddenly realized that I was pouring my present, my life today, into the past—into recording or remembering things that have already happened. I don't want my marriage to be over, but it is. Even sadder is the fact that I have no vision for what is ahead. No dreams, no wants, nothing. I am a blank. So I said to myself, 'You have got to get a life.'"

Though I expected a smile from Margaret's light choice of words, tears brimmed. She took a deep breath and continued. "I love seeing my kids, but they have their own lives now and something in me is saying that I should, too—have a separate life, I mean. Thankfully, Todd left me well enough off financially that I'm not forced to work, but really, right now work sounds pretty good. I'm only fifty years old and I am just filling my days with things I don't really care about. Good things, but not things that matter a lot to *me*. I do this for this person and that for that one, more busyness than real satisfaction." She paused again, just long enough to catch her breath.

"Then I thought, *How selfish!* and I started down that old familiar path of beating myself up for wanting anything for myself. Interestingly, though, the verse that came to mind was the one about Jesus' yoke and burden being easy and light. My life feels anything but easy or light. Do I sound ungrateful?"

"No," I replied. "You sound like a woman in a lot of pain. Maybe you are birthing something new."

"Well if I am, I have no idea what," my friend replied with a frustrated sigh. "I thought, *Okay, what can I do? What are my gifts? What do I want to do?* Easy questions, right? I've asked them of my kids for years! But I came up with nothing. A big fat zero. I have a degree in fashion design, but I hate it. I couldn't care less about fashion, and I *hate* to sew. Who would have guessed? Even worse, I've never even admitted that to myself until last week. And this scrapbooking thing that I have spent *years* doing is not really a personal passion at all. But you'd never know that, would you? I know I'm good at it. But I give them all away because I don't really care much about them. It's as if I am just unthinkingly doing something to pass the time. What is the matter with me?"

"Now, wait a minute," I interrupted. "Don't be so hard on yourself. You've had a really tough five years."

"Oh, it gets worse. After I wrote down the question 'What are my gifts?' I started thinking. *Gifts? Who do you think you are? You are just an average housewife. Your life is spent. It's too late for you.*" My friend physically shuddered as she recalled the deeply painful moment. "I don't know where that voice came from, and it was *mean* . . . not a nice little curiosity. It was like an accusation with claws; saying that I was nothing and would always be nothing; that my life was over, trivial, a trivial pursuit.

"And I didn't even have an answer for the question *Who do you think you are?* So I just stopped. It was just too hard." Margaret's voice cracked, feeling again an aching despair. Continuing almost in a whisper, she said, "But when I stopped, I felt that same horrid, empty feeling that started this whole thing. It was awful. I'm not sure I ever want to look at a scrapbook again . . . *or* a journal." Then with an attempted laugh, she turned to me. "Now fix me, will you?"

Stilled and silenced by my friend's perplexing realizations and raw pain, I grabbed her hand as we sat together in silence for a long time.

Lot's Wife

Remember Lot's wife? She's the one who turned into a pillar of salt. To set the scene, Lot, Abraham's nephew, was in the process of being rescued by angels from Sodom, one of two wicked cities God intended to destroy in the very near future.

[Lot] hesitated, the men [angels] grasped his hand and the hands of his wife and of his two daughters and led them safely out of the city, for the Lord was merciful to them. As soon as they had brought them out, one of them said, "Flee for your lives! Don't look back, and don't stop anywhere in the plain! Flee to the mountains or you will be swept away!" . . . But Lot's wife looked back, and she became a pillar of salt. (Genesis 19:16–17, 26)

Her Past Was Killing Her

Most of us want to believe that we live our lives in a fairly self-aware, consciously chosen fashion. Unfortunately, in the busyness and noise of our culture, that is often not the case. Self-awareness is a particular challenge for many women. With our nurturing nature, we can probably tell you what every person in the room (or at least in our family) needs and perhaps even what they want, where they excel, and what they might be struggling with, but we usually cannot answer those questions for ourselves.

If you relate to that assertion, you may not be surprised when I say that many women live fairly miserable lives and never even notice! They are living the only life they have imagined. Though some in the church may call a lack of self-awareness a moral success, I don't think such oblivion is God's idea of wisdom, and have rarely seen it produce anything akin to the fruit of God's Spirit: love, joy, peace . . . (Galatians 5:22–23).

It seems that such a gap between perception and reality may have been the case with Lot's wife. She seemed to be attached to a life and a city that she may not have thought much about, or at least not evaluated with much wisdom.

God's assessment was such that he sent angels to destroy it: *"The outcry to the Lord against its people is so great that he has sent us to destroy it"* (Genesis 19:13). No wonder the angel said, *"Flee for your lives!"*

Yet she seemed quite attached to her life there . . . understandably attached. *Home.* The idea of home is a powerfully magnetic force in women. For many, it is our center. We love the familiarity, even if it becomes a harmful place for our souls. We so want to define whatever we experience at home—the good, the bad, and the ugly—as normal.

Accepting the truth that our home may actually be a place from which we should "run for our lives" can be a first step toward new growth. We know that the alternative unknown life might be even more frightening. On the other hand, it may also be our salvation.

Her Only Escape Was Unknown Territory

The instructions of the angels were clear: Flee, don't look back, don't stop in the plains, go all the way to the mountains. With the travel limitations of that day and time, Lot's wife likely knew nothing of the life she was being called to in the mountains. At least the plains were familiar. She could see them from Sodom.

In his book *Becoming Human,* Brian Taylor describes how often we want restoration rather than transformation. We want God to simply tweak our lives, make us into a new and improved version of the woman we already know, nothing too dramatic. Yet we serve a God who is all about transformation: turning caterpillars into butterflies, making the new pretty unrecognizable to the old. God tells us not to stop in the plains but go all the way to the mountains, the land of the unknown. We are not to settle for simply living a good life, we are called to shine.[2]

The real irony for us as Christians is that this kind of leap into the unknown is the very nature of the life of faith we are called to live as our *norm*. Faith moves us toward that which we cannot see: *"Now faith is confidence in what we hope for and assurance about what we do not see"* (Hebrews 11:1). "Not seeing" is both an uncomfortable and essential prerequisite. Considering the priority God places on personal transformation, often the thing we cannot see is a yet-to-be-known version of ourselves!

She Mistook Her Past for Her Life

Remember Lot's wife! Whoever tries to keep their life will lose it, and whoever loses their life will preserve it. (Luke 17:32–33)

Many scholars say that the best commentary we find on Scripture is another portion of Scripture. This New Testament reference to the story of Lot's wife is a small illustration sandwiched in the middle of a section speaking of the time when the kingdom of God comes suddenly to earth. The message of this illustration is clear: If you try to plant yourself in the past—save your life as you define it now—you will lose it. But if you take this leap, if you let go of your life as it is, as you know it, you will be saved. This is not presented as a nice option but rather an essential element of our faith journey.

The Christian life is one that we are called to live in forward motion. Sometimes, though, we get stuck in a rut without realizing it. One common way we avoid the transformative, shining life we have been called to live is to become caught in what I call the unimagined life. As wonderfully gifted nurturers, we can get lost in fulfilling the dreams and agendas of others and never even think about what God might have in mind for our particular lives—beyond taking care of those we love. We choose to live passively, responsively, without personal vision, investment, or creativity. Or for those who may dare to sense God's unique calling, it can become a call we never get around to answering. We struggle to *find* time for our own hopes and dreams, never thinking to *take* or *make* the time. As the saying goes, "A woman's work is never done." Let's face it: It's less risky to operate from someone else's vision, passion, and plan.

So many factors work against our visionary initiative. It is a human tendency to become stuck and to build ruts. Understandably, the better the life, the greater the temptation to preserve it as is. Remember the rich young ruler (Matthew 19:16–30). When the flow of our life is good, we want to institutionalize whatever has brought that goodness. We want to turn our living God into a fixed idol. At times, we try to hold on to the goodness of one phase of life by simply not acknowledging that it is gone.

We may cling to our offspring as children though they have grown to adulthood. We may cling to our professional identity when we sense new desires and perhaps even a call to become more focused at home. We refuse to consider remarriage though our spouse has long been deceased. We complain if the music changes at church or the furniture is moved because the way it was worked so well for us for so long. We pour concrete around all that is good (or bad!), including our souls, and turn the living into the dead. Thus we sabotage the unseeable and brilliant goodness God has imagined for us.

Often a passive failure on our part to continually reimagine our lives is applauded by friends and family. The reality of family systems is that our change or growth could force others members to change as well. A more creative agenda might well ask for some appropriate compromise of their plans. Not to mention the fact that most of us have already filled our lives with doing good things.

Margaret's scrapbooks were truly treasures for her family and would be sorely missed if she ceased to create them. My guess is that Lot's wife had friends within her city, people she cared for and who cared for her. It is hard enough to move toward the unknown and doubly difficult if that movement causes those we love pain or loss. Yet as relationally messy as it may be, the Christian life is one we are called to live in forward motion, not mistaking our past for our life.

By Clinging to Her Past, She Lost Her Life

Lot's wife was led by the hand out of town, but once on her own, she turned to look back and became a pillar of salt. All her color, her unique beauty and vivacity, disappeared. She lost her life. One of the most difficult aspects of this kind of tragedy is that we never see the life that was missed. Sin is sometimes categorized in two ways: sins of omission (good works we fail to do) and sins of commission (wrong things done). Sins of commission are easy to spot: lying, stealing, cheating (to name a few). Sins of omission are more difficult to see and therefore to own. Losing our lives or even a less dramatic refusal to shine is a sin of omission. A good act never done is by definition something that does not exist. It is elusive and hard to grasp or count as loss to the kingdom.

Nevertheless, many of us feel or sense that loss even when we cannot see it. Think of the empty feeling Margaret experienced as she placed her latest scrapbook on the shelf. The description of her life as a trivial pursuit was not bound up in what she had done (nurturing her family, fashion design, scrapbooking) as much as in the *absence* of the fullness of what God had called her to do. Another woman may well be called and find deep satisfaction in scrapbooking and fashion design. The presence or absence of such deep satisfaction is an important part of discernment. In Proverbs, it is said about Lady Wisdom, *"She senses that her gain is good"* (31:18, NASB).

A good example of one who listened well to such internal and telling satisfaction was Eric Liddell, whose story was told in the movie *Chariots of Fire.* Eric was the son of missionary parents and a very talented runner. His sister viewed running as a trivial pursuit, unworthy of Eric's time and attention. She projected her calling and sensibilities onto her brother. Eric saw things differently. In a conversation with his sister, he said, "I believe God made me for a purpose, but he also made me fast, and when I run I feel God's pleasure." And later, "To give up running would be to hold [God] in contempt."[3] Wise discernment comes not from some objective value we or others may place on any given task but from the willingness to listen to the voice and calling of God within our unique gifts, passions, and experiences.

Lot's wife's limited imagination became a destructive force in her life. She saw herself only as a woman who lived in Sodom, a vision that created a direct conflict with God's calling to leave that place. She makes me think of a woman I know who will not leave her openly abusive husband because she cannot see herself as an unmarried woman. Another woman is inappropriately involved with her adult sons because she cannot imagine herself void of the task of active mothering. An elderly friend is resisting relocating to be closer to her children because she cannot imagine leaving the only home she has known in the last fifty years. God calls us forward, but to grow is frightening because within that invitation lies an identity crisis of sometimes massive proportions: a God-ordained death and resurrection that is meant to build a life of faith and transform all who dare.

Margaret (continued)

After several minutes of heavy silence, Margaret spoke again with a deep sigh, "But it isn't true. I know it's not true. Even though I don't know who I am or what I'm passionate about, I am not a zero. And as far as I know, my life is not even close to over. There is hope. I want to live my life forward. This trip is step one. Though I have no idea how it is step one," she said with a genuine laugh. With the intention of changing the subject, Margaret opened her bag and pulled out a current issue of *Biochemical Genetics* magazine.

"I see you brought along a little light reading material. What in the world are you doing with that magazine?" I continued in her lighter vein.

"Do you mean to tell me that I've never told you what a hound I am about genetics?" Margaret began. I soon discovered that my friend had nurtured a secret passion for decades! I knew she was smart, but *genetics*?

I asked, "So why didn't you major in *that* in college?"

Margaret replied, "I thought about it, and my high school biology teacher practically begged me to. But when I talked to my mom; goodness, I even remember the conversation. She said, 'Oh honey, now look . . . think about this for a minute. Who do you think you are? You aren't George Washington Carver; you're a *girl*! Just stick to fashion, dear; you've got a good plan.' So I never said, or even *thought,* another word about it."

"Did you hear what you just said?" I noted.

"What do you mean?" Margaret replied.

" *'Who do you think you are?'* Does that ring any bells? I think I hear an echo from your journal," I observed.

"You're kidding. From way back then? I don't know . . . I don't know . . . maybe so," Margaret replied with a new curiosity.

A timely update...

You will be happy to hear that Margaret is finishing her biology degree next month, has already presented her latest genetics research at a national conference, and is deciding between three PhD programs that are vying to pay her while she continues her research! Who knew?

Your Story

1. Do you connect with Margaret's story? How is yours similar? Different? Do you connect with the story of Lot's wife? How is your story different? Similar?

2. Are there aspects of your "home" past or present that have done damage to your beauty and goodness? Have you adopted, internalized, or normalized any of those patterns in such a way that they sabotage your growth forward?

3. Make a list of ten words that others would say describe you. Now make a list of ten things you would say about yourself. Prayerfully examine your lists, asking God to help you see if each characteristic is the real you or the echo of an imposed identity from the past.

4. Think back to your girlhood dreams. Who did you want to be? What did you want to do? Where did you want to go? Name three dreams. What do they tell you about yourself both then and now? Note any emotional responses to this exercise.

5. Chart the course of each dream. Is it still alive? Did it fold into another? Did it die? Would the death be described as one from natural causes or was it by disease or "murder"? Describe the scene or the disease process. What part of you was left behind?

6. What is your emotional response to the quote that began this chapter: "And now you must go out into your heart as onto a vast plain . . ."

7. Write out a story or make a collage of a moment in your life when you dared to venture out onto that vast plain or elected to remain in a more known place. Do you see that moment in new ways?

2

The Unworthy Life

*Love and belonging are essential to the human
experience. As I conducted my interviews, I realized
that only one thing separated the men and women
who felt a deep sense of love and belonging from
the people who seemed to struggle for it. That
one thing is the belief in their worthiness.*[1]

BRENE BROWN

*But God demonstrates his own love for us in this:
While we were still sinners, Christ died for us.*

ROMANS 5:8

CONSIDER: Take a full minute to become still. From that settled,
listening place, prayerfully call to mind one experience from your
life that caused you to bury some part of your story or some aspect
of yourself.

Cathy

I first met Cathy when we were both in nursing school. She was a petite blonde with a passion for surgery. Clearly, surgical nursing was a good fit for her: A perfectionist by nature with an amazing capacity for detail, no aspect of care escaped her rapt attention. Both her academics and personal appearance reflected the same precision. She was a straight-A student and the most beautiful young woman in our class. I couldn't imagine how she found time for it all. I knew she studied way into the night, and she once told me she got up at four-something every morning to get ready for a 6:45 shift at the hospital. I could only admire her dedication and the results of it.

Though we lost touch after school, our paths crossed again a few years ago when we found ourselves registering our daughters for the same ballet class. I have to admit that I didn't recognize her right away. It wasn't so much the twenty years as the large amount of weight she had put on. Delighted to reconnect but too busy that day for a real conversation, we agreed to meet for coffee the next week while the girls danced.

We began to restore our friendship with ease. About two months later, Cathy brought up the weight issue: "I surprised you, didn't I?" She went on to recount a part of her story that stunned me even more. She told me that when I had known her before, she had been in the throes of an eating disorder. "It began when I was in my teens. They say it's connected to the fact that I was sexually abused as a child. You know, you're the first person, besides my husband and my counselor, I've ever told."

I was so surprised. "Oh my, Cathy. I had no idea. You always looked so perfectly put together. You were the envy of us all!"

"I know . . . but my perfectionism isn't an asset, believe me. There was something in me that said it was the only way I could survive. I felt so, so, so awful and dirty inside. I thought that if I was perfect on the outside maybe people would put up with me, tolerate me. Isn't it ironic? I felt like I was just barely getting by, living my whole life as a continual apology, and you thought I had it all together!"

"Ironic, yes, and so sad," I added.

"Well, things did get better for me. I got some counseling. But unfortunately, as the eating disorder improved, I started slowly putting on this weight. I guess I'm not a very well-balanced person. I'm beginning to think I just traded one problem for another."

Cathy now managed a large surgery practice for several physicians. She was continuing with counseling and began to attend a weight-loss program at a local church. Over several months, it was fabulous to see her petite frame begin to reappear. Then suddenly things began to shift and the weight loss became weight gain. At our weekly outings, her routine decaf skinny latte became a triple-shot mocha fudge Frappuccino.

This time, she did not bring up the subject for conversation. After a few weeks, I rallied my courage, took a deep breath, and said, "Okay, Cathy. What happened to the weight-loss plan?"

"I don't know," she replied, then continuing quickly, almost blurting out the story before she could change her mind, she said, "About a month ago, I bought myself a really beautiful new suit. I had lost five pounds that week and wanted to reward myself. You know, that weight-loss stuff is hard work. I looked so great in it." She dropped her eyes and grinned a little. I wasn't sure if it was genuine pleasure or a contemptuous smirk.

Without looking up she continued, "The next morning I woke up and thought I'd wear it to work. I was standing in front of the mirror and then from out of the blue came this thought: *Just who do you think you are? Who are you kidding? You are worthless, damaged goods. You can dress up all you please; you'll never be worth a thing.* She covered her mouth with her hand, stopped to catch her breath, almost choking as her throat tightened, and said in a whisper, almost despairingly, "So I thought, *Why try?*" Her voice was thick with self-contempt and despair. Her eyes were still lowered and brimming tears, evidencing her unspeakable heartache.

The Woman Caught in Adultery

In a story involving something as seemingly black and white as adultery, at times we need to dig deeper and listen more closely to mine the real story beneath the surface action. In this case, we can gain new insight by reading the story a little backward. First, let's read it as written.

The religion scholars and Pharisees led in a woman who had been caught in an act of adultery. They stood her in plain sight of everyone and said, "Teacher, this woman was caught red-handed in the act of adultery. Moses, in the Law, gives orders to stone such persons. What do you say?" They were trying to trap him into saying something incriminating so they could bring charges against him.

Jesus bent down and wrote with his finger in the dirt. They kept at him, badgering him. He straightened up and said, "The sinless one among you, go first: Throw the stone." Bending down again, he wrote some more in the dirt.

Hearing that, they walked away, one after another, beginning with the oldest. The woman was left alone. Jesus stood up and spoke to her. "Woman, where are they? Does no one condemn you?"

"No one, Master."

"Neither do I," said Jesus. "Go on your way. From now on, don't sin." (John 8:3–11 THE MESSAGE)

Guilty Without Defense?

When most of us read this story for the first time, we assume that the adulteress is guilty and without defense, right? That may be so. But if we elect to read this story more closely, we need to factor in a few cultural realities. Such as: Women in that culture had very little power of any kind. Therefore, almost any relationship with a man contained a significant and inherent power differential. Even in our modern society power differentials exist. Think of adult female employees who have affairs with their bosses or college students who have sexual encounters with teachers or clients who become involved with therapists. Social and legal systems recognize the relational power differential as an unavoidable influence on the dynamic of choice. So much so that even if this woman chose the affair, determining her culpability is tricky. Even as an adult decision on her part, with the cultural reality of powerlessness, that choice might also be victimization. Such a complex and compassionate consideration is bolstered by the fact that Jesus never specifically addressed the issue of adultery with her.

A Pawn in a Larger Game

Another reality we need to factor into our reading of this text is the fact that this woman was clearly a pawn in a larger game. Anytime we become an object for another's use or pleasure rather than a subject in mutual relationship, we become a victim. This woman was an object being used and abused by the religious scholars and Pharisees. The gospel writer makes sure we know they have a specific purpose for this moment; concern for her is nowhere on their radar screen. And of course Jesus didn't miss this important reality.

The fact that the offending man was not brought with her also gives us pause. Some have suggested that the whole scene was just a little too convenient, a setup from the start with the man as coconspirator. For many in the righteously indignant crowd, this woman was more object than subject, more issue than person, more theological agenda than one made in God's image.

So, to backtrack, we have a woman who may be a sinner with regard to adultery, or may be the powerless victim of a sexual predator or a setup. In either case, she is clearly a victim of abuse by these religious tricksters. Maybe this isn't such a cut-and-dried story after all.

The Sin Beneath the Sin

One thing we do know is that if she had a choice in the affair, the course she chose was a self-destructive one. Affairs are always no-win situations, always a decision to settle for less than the goodness of a committed marriage relationship that God has ordained. Additionally, in that culture at that time, to choose an affair was not simply settling for less, it meant opening yourself to the possibility of being stoned to death!

Now, this is where I think we benefit from reading the story backward. Jesus possessed the wisdom and compassion to address the most critical, most destructive, deepest sin issue at hand in this situation. Even as he cleverly and wisely dealt with these men, he would not cooperate with their inhumane regard for this woman who stood before him. He would move toward her to love and to heal. So looking at what Jesus did and said will be our best clue as to where the roots of her possible choice for adultery are hidden, where the sin beneath the sin lay.

A Nonverbal Clue

Though the woman is often pictured in a heap on the ground, the text actually says that they stood her in their midst. She was standing. So what was the first thing Jesus did? He stooped down. He bent low enough to be able to write in the dirt with his finger. I imagine that her eyes were downcast; she was likely shaking in fear. Remember, these men might well have already had stones in their hands, stones meant to end her life.

Jesus quite possibly lowered himself into her line of sight. He joined her. He did not stand above, but below, communicating his heart of compassion with his body. He let her know that she was not alone; that he saw her pain and humiliation and joined her there. Did she dare look into his eyes? He stood for a moment to address the haranguing crowd, and then stooped again. She seemed to be much more his concern than these crafty men. But what exactly was he seeking to communicate to her? What would salvation, healing, forgiveness, or repentance look like for this woman?

A Different Kind of Confession

Once they were alone, Jesus stood and spoke to her, asking her two questions: *"Woman, where are they? Does no one condemn you?"* It seems significant to me that he approached her with questions instead of statements, possibly wanting to invite her to speak. Perhaps he was soliciting a confession of sorts—a life-giving, life-altering confession. Certainly not the kind of confession one might expect if this woman were viewed as a "simple adulteress." No, the confession he sought was this: *"No one, Master."* He wanted her to say, to speak the reality, that she was not less than the others. She was not worth less than anyone else. No one, not even the most "righteous" men she knew, could condemn her.

So if that was the healing confession, what was the destructive issue at hand? What was the sin beneath the sin? Could it be that her core sin was the belief that she was worth less than others? *Worthless?* Might her self-contempt be the hidden sin? Could it be that her lack of acknowledging her God-given worth and dignity as a woman was the root of her choice for adultery? As we noted earlier, a choice for sexual immorality is a choice for less than the goodness God desires for us. It evidences a tragic loss of vision and a deadly loss of hope for goodness. At the very least, a self-image of being "unworthy" in regard to others would make her vulnerable to that kind of compromise.

Self-contempt is a critical and crippling spiritual issue for many women. I have seen it so often that I feel as if it is a part of our DNA. In this instance, we also know that this woman was being treated as an object, abused by the men who brought her. Such experiences of being treated with contempt, objectification, and true victimization reinforce false beliefs about our value. Every time we suffer that kind of inhumane treatment, we are tempted to let such unjust suffering define us. When we are treated as if we are worthless, our errant self-contempt is emboldened.

And when we choose self-contempt, we choose a path that leads to death. This is the path of the living apology. On the inside is unbridled self-hatred so strong that hope for noble and good personal human connection is lost. Instead, we focus our energy on earning relationship or a *sense* of relationship, establishing a facade of worth, never really believing we are worthy. The best we can hope for is to fool some of the people some of the time.

Authenticity becomes the enemy. We earn relationship through being the best and the most or the least and the lowly. We become the best looking or the most funny. We are the girls most likely to take a dare for the entertainment of others or give our bodies to satisfy others' passions or suffer abuse in silence. We are the ones who go over and above all expectation, to extreme lengths, to be there for friends. We have little concept of self, much less wise self-protection. Self-respect does not exist. We'll do whatever we need to, good or bad, to stay connected. As ones who are "worth less," it seems like our only option.

We are often so full of self-hatred that we become numb to it, sometimes even inviting abuse from others or choosing blatant self-destruction to perpetuate this false belief and keep hope at bay. As we disregard and lose hope in our own God-given worth, we sin against God and ourselves. The inner suffering of such hopelessness is often even more painful than whatever external compromises and consequential suffering we may face.

A New Way of Life

Jesus knew that in this moment this woman's heart needed healing more than her behavior needed shaping. Only after dealing with this root issue would this woman's life truly be different. Offering her healing from the inside out, with a few words, Jesus not only addresses the core issues of sin with others, but he also offers complete forgiveness: " *'Neither do I [condemn you],' said Jesus. 'Go on your way. From now on, don't sin.'* "

Jesus' nonspecific exhortation ("don't sin") intrigues me. Certainly we know he no longer wants her to engage in adultery, but perhaps he also wants her to let go of the conviction that she is unworthy of relationship with others who surround her. She is worthy because God has given her worth, and no sin, no victimization, can take that away. His words seem to invite and empower her to live a life free from condemnation, to go *her* way in fullness and radiance and to give up the familiar, corrosive, and sinful pattern of apologizing for her existence.

Imagine the difference. Imagine a woman who believed that she was no longer "worth less," one whose presence could *stand eye-to-eye* in the presence of even the most religious leaders of her city. Imagine a woman who knew Jesus had seen her most sinful and destructive choices of both heart and behavior and joined her with love, forgiveness, and a vision for a new, different way of life. Imagine a woman who could carry the story of her suffering and very public humiliation with her head held high, acknowledging it all as a part of her story without letting it define her for a minute. Imagine a woman who knew that neither her wounds nor her sin had even for a moment diminished the worth and beauty of her feminine soul.

Cathy (continued)

The day Cathy told me about her sense of being "worthless, damaged goods" was a profoundly sad day for both of us. We cried together over coffee, not really caring who might be watching. I knew her self-contempt was deeply rooted and that I couldn't just say "it isn't so" and all would be well. This present pain revealed a whole new level of healing that needed to happen. But how does one leave such a past behind? Or undo such core convictions about identity? Or is there another way?

When we got together the next week, Cathy told me how her path had begun to shift in healing directions. "I don't quite understand it, but somehow, just saying that 'worthless, damaged goods' thing out loud helped. I said it and I survived it. And you didn't run away or hate me. Those awful words have been roaming around inside me for God knows how long. And even as I was saying it, I think a part of me knew it wasn't true. I am damaged. And I *was* treated like worthless goods, but that doesn't make me worthless. That's not all of who I am."

Cathy continued, "For so long, I worked so hard to make sure all that ugliness stayed buried way, way, way deep. The memories of the abuse, the self-hatred, that really massive sense of being worth less than nothing—I thought the only way to deal with it was to bury it *and* be so good on the outside that no one would ever even suspect it was there.

"When I had to face the eating disorder just so I could live, I thought maybe religion was the trick. I wanted forgiveness to magically fix it all somehow, to *undo* it, make it not so. When I did counseling work years ago on forgiveness, I really did make good progress. And I thought I was done. Maybe that's it; I thought it was over. I forgave my abuser. All that work was real, just not enough. I had dealt with my abuser; I had never dealt with *me*. I had no idea about all these ideas swirling around in my head. I guess now I need to forgive *me* for being so abusive to *me*. My abuse is a part of my story, but it is not who I am." Cathy's voice was stronger and more sure than I had ever heard it. As she continued, tears, which seemed to be tears of gratitude, came to her eyes.

"For the first time I can actually imagine myself moving forward, beyond this pain. Who will I be without it? Or no, maybe that's not the question. Who will I be *with* it as just a part of who I am?"

Your *Story*

1. Do you connect with Cathy's story? How is yours similar? Different? Do you connect with the story of the woman caught in adultery? How is your story different? Similar?

2. Are there any parts of your story that you have difficulty acknowledging even in the presence of people you trust?

3. Have you ever been treated like an object? Describe the moment. Did that experience leave any lasting impressions or scripts with you?

4. What self-contemptuous accusations do you hear inside your head most often? Are any of those connected to parts of your story that are difficult to acknowledge?

5. What contexts, circumstances, or situations seem to cause you to feel worth less than others? Recall and describe three specific scenes in as much detail as possible (color, light, sound, smell, words, textures, time of day, season). What were you hearing inside at those moments?

6. When, where, and with whom does the fullest, most authentic expression of *you* surface?

7. Describe yourself as a whole and worthy woman. Use words or images, perhaps even a collage. Be careful to prayerfully integrate the parts of your life or experience that you might be tempted to judge unworthy or unacceptable, perhaps the experience you named in the invitation to "consider" at the opening of this chapter. Do all the parts of your story fit? Which do, which do not?

8. As a whole woman, how do you regard the parts of your story you once avoided?

3

The Unlived Life

You didn't tell me how bad it was.
You didn't tell me that I nearly died.
Amidst all the work, the fury,
   the haste,
With all the excitement, the plans,
   the hopes—
I nearly died
A death not known, not believed in—
That would have been the horror of it.
Nothing told me.
No one spoke.
And in my dying that no one saw,
I was applauded.
All was mine—the laughter, the smiles,
The adulation,
Stored and gathered,
They were mine.
Only rarely, my spirit disturbed,
I would be sad and wonder.
And then with dash and scorn

I would dismiss
This weakness!
See my work! See my achievement!
Don't these speak for me?
When so many smiled upon me,
So many admired
How could I die?
But in the years you disturbed me,
God;
All were sure, except you.
No one told me
I was dying. . . .[1]

EDWINA GATELEY

CONSIDER: Reflect on any areas of your heart that carry a sense of deadness: a relationship, a loss, a dream, a season, a place, or even a part of your body. Give yourself the freedom to notice the deadness without judgment or the need to explain, defend, or even understand it.

My Story

How can a woman get to age thirty-five without a sense of who she is apart from what she does? Sadly, it's easier than you might think. From kindergarten on I was a teacher's pet. And from ninth grade on, a super-achiever spiritually as well.

I have a distinct memory of being in our junior high parking lot, waiting for my mom after driver's education. I was thinking through my life. "So I'll make good grades in high school and go to a good college. And make good grades there and get a good job. And marry a good guy. And have a good family. And die. Is that all there is to life?" You might say I was a deep thinker early on.

By age sixteen, I was sitting on a friend's living room floor taking notes from a Navigator college ministry team leader from the University of Texas-Austin. He gave lectures on Scripture, Prayer, Eternal Perspective (my deep thinker parts loved this one!), and many other topics. He taught us how to do chapter analysis Bible study and how to read our Bibles and pray daily. I soaked it all up and more once I was in college at the same university, involved with the same group of folks. My Friday nights, to my great enjoyment, were spent doing Bible study, and then sleeping in preparation for an early Saturday morning study.

In those days, I learned a lot of Scripture and a lot about God. My life revolved completely around doing and thinking. I had no tolerance for stillness or emotion or anything girly. I valued efficiency, purpose, and right belief. If someone had asked me about my internal world, I would not have known what to say. In fact, as I write these words, I remember a kind professor in my last semester of nursing school expressing genuine concern about my emotional health, or lack thereof, and my "drivenness." I was so clueless that although I recorded her words at one level, the possibility that her observations might have merit never occurred to me. The church affirmed my life of doing and that was good enough for me.

And so it continued for many years—almost two decades. By my early thirties, I had been married to my husband, Bob, for ten years and was mom to three children, Bobby (eight), Jenna (five), and Betsy (two). We were very involved in a small Bible church, as were almost all of our friends. I taught Sunday school, directed VBS, mentored women, and was devoted to intercessory prayer. I was also an active part of the leadership in a community Bible study for women.

My discipline was strong and I was still driven. My calendar was packed. My mind was full and clear: There were lots of answers, few questions, and little uncertainty allowed. Proper discipline was my primary concern with my children. My emotions, as far as I knew, were gratefully nonexistent. I remember telling a girlfriend on the phone one day that I had no idea why women had to be so emotional; it just got in the way of doing good things for God. (*Ugh* . . . I would eat those words.) In spiritual gifts inventories, I would score high on leadership and teaching abilities and very low on the gift of mercy.

Yet there were three things I could not fix to my satisfaction: my body, my career path, and my marriage. After struggling with severe sciatica with each of my three pregnancies, I now had lingering pain down my right leg. Despite numerous attempts at resolution and wearing a lift in my shoe, I continued to have pain. My solution was not to think about it. Mind over matter; problem solved.

That same solution also worked pretty well in arena #2: my career. Though I had a degree in nursing, I did not enjoy the time I spent using it. I just knew, somehow, that I was more gifted at being a corporate executive than a mom. Keeping those kids in line was a struggle. With the pace of my daily schedule, it was easy to leave those concerns to future years.

My marriage angst was less easy to ignore. If only my husband would be more romantic, I was sure this hole in my heart would go away. After all, it was his duty, his moral obligation to satisfy my soul. Yes, that was it! It was all his fault. But apart from the big hole in my soul, we were pretty compatible and otherwise focused on church and kids. After all, no one said marriage would be easy; it's a commitment that builds character, right? I had gone into it expecting to serve 100 percent, so in many ways it was just what I imagined. Never mind that hole.

In 1990, my husband got word that the refinery where he worked was closing. After looking at various possibilities, we made the leap and moved to the U.S. Virgin Island of St. Croix. The job looked promising, and we had always wanted to live overseas. Of course, from my perspective, it was all about duty, not beauty. It was the mission field, not a resort island in the Caribbean. I actively made plans to begin a Bible study class once we were settled.

God had other plans. We joined a small church, but the study group did not work out. Life was so much simpler in the Caribbean: If Woolworth's didn't have it in stock it was not to be had. You simply adapted. And once you'd seen the island's seven-mile by twenty-seven-mile span, you'd seen it all. Productivity and efficiency were not highly valued on this small island. People invested in relationships—not things, experiences, events, or doing. I enjoyed coffee with my neighbor Elizabeth every day as the kids played after school. I discovered new hobbies: gardening and golf. I soaked up the sun, and slowly—day by sunshiny day—the pace of my life and rhythm of my heart began to soften and shift.

I was more ready for change than I knew. I remember no frustration at all as my three-year-old, Betsy, and I slowly and methodically went to three different stores each week to buy produce, milk, and dry goods—and a fourth for bread. The beauty of the island never ceased to catch my breath—every time I caught a glimpse of the turquoise water. Something tender and fresh began to grow inside of me, but I was not at all sure what it was. I felt both more relaxed and more alive. Colors were brighter, music more melodious. Something new was happening in me that felt both good and unfamiliar, beyond my understanding, much less language. On island time, there was no rush to figure it out.

Of course, not everything was better. Working an enormous number of hours in a crazy, stressful job, my husband was still not tending that hole in my heart. In fact, two years later he was burned-out. It was time for us to leave. Though not one to cry, I wept inexplicably and uncontrollably the day we departed. And although I didn't know what was happening to me, I knew that on that island, in that community, something had come alive in me and I was desperate to hold on to it even though I did not understand it.

Martha

Scripture offers three narratives in which the sisters Mary and Martha of Bethany are mentioned. Many of us struggle to remember that the Gospels are not necessarily chronological in their recording of Jesus' life and ministry. Nevertheless, it seems safe to assume the sequence of these stories. Until recently, I had not thought of them as a single narrative of growth in these women, each event connecting to the others in important ways.

Full Hands, Empty Heart

Notice first what this story says about the quality of Martha's relationships.

As Jesus and his disciples were on their way, he came to a village where a woman named Martha opened her home to him. She had a sister called Mary, who sat at the Lord's feet listening to what he said. But Martha was distracted by all the preparations that had to be made. She came to him and asked, "Lord, don't you care that my sister has left me to do the work by myself? Tell her to help me!"

"Martha, Martha," the Lord answered, "you are worried and upset about many things, but few things are needed—or indeed only one. Mary has chosen what is better, and it will not be taken away from her." (Luke 10:38–42)

In short, at least two of Martha's important relationships were a mess. She was judgmental, and likely angry with Mary for not helping, and she accused Jesus of not caring for her because he had not corrected Mary's neglect. Martha was relating to both Jesus and Mary through the narrow lens of moral duty. Notice the imperative statements and accusations rather than curiosity, the demands instead of requests.

Martha knew that her own hands were way too full. At the same time, her accusations reveal that her heart felt way too empty, not cared for. Like the woman in the opening poem, she did not realize that she was sensing her own dying. She was seeking to fix something that was huge in her life and very wrong—like you might seek to fix a rusty engine. Since duty was her only lens, it must be a duty problem. Since she was maxed out on her end, it must be the fault of Mary and Jesus. She spoke of the neglect of both as an assumed moral obligation. She said nothing about her feelings or her relationships, only her work.

Martha's vision was smaller than Jesus desired for her and focused in an unhelpful direction. I hear grief in his voice as he invites her into a heart-to-heart relationship. *"Martha, Martha,"* he said, compassionately reflecting back to her the anxiety and the stress he saw in her eyes and heard in her words. He was calling her back to relationship, helping her to become present in her circumstances. Like so many of us, Martha was so focused on *doing* that she did not recognize the state of her *being*.

As I read Jesus' words, I can see Martha's lips stiffen and her thoughts race: *You bet I'm worried and bothered. There are things to get done that just aren't getting done. I have good reason to be upset!* (Been there, said that!) But he continues, *"Few things are needed. . . . Mary has chosen what is better."* I see her expression becoming confused, perplexed. Jesus seeks to broaden her lens beyond duty and societal scripts of unthinking service, knowing that that they can never give her life or fill her hurting heart.

She Missed the Better Part

Christians sometimes forget that Jesus is all about the good news of God. He says his yoke is easy and his burden light. He has come that we might have full joy. He comes to us bringing peace, his peace. He has come to bring life, abundant life. The fruit of his Spirit is love, joy, peace, patience, goodness, kindness, gentleness, faithfulness, and self-control . . . things against which there are certainly no laws (Galatians 5:22–23). He did not want Martha (or us) to be worried or bothered by anything.

Sometimes we interpret Mary's choice of the better part as a moral failure on Martha's part. Perhaps on some level it is; but it is more like a tragic missing of the mark, missing the good part. Martha did not understand that the work of

God in her life offered sweetness, goodness, the good part—*life* rather than a longer to-do list. Of course, God has also planned good works for us to do, but to only see the *work* before us is a kind of blindness that distorts the essence of our relationship with God.

In her narrow, duty-first view, Martha reduced herself to more ministry machine than beloved human being; and she attempted to pull Mary into the same error. In this mindset, Martha was sabotaging the very essence of the life Jesus was offering. When she turned her relationship with him into a mathematical equation of moral obligation, she began to unlive the vital life he offered. Martha's busyness was more a symptom of her misguided blindness than the problem itself.

Right Confession, Wrong Focus

I would also suggest that the next story in our series of three reveals shades of the same narrow vision and misplaced focus. This is the story of the death and resurrection of Lazarus, recorded chiefly through the experience of his sisters. You may want to read the whole story (John 11:1–43) before continuing since we have included only portions here.

The story began when the two sisters sent for Jesus after their brother Lazarus became ill. Banking on all they knew of Jesus' healing powers and the strength of their friendship, they expected an immediate response. Though Jesus was in a city not far away, they heard nothing. Lazarus died and was buried. Then Jesus showed up.

Once more, Martha was in pain, this time because of the death of her brother. And once more she tried to fix her pain in a way that was more precept than person focused. Here I see Martha not as a duty-focused production machine, but a computer seeking new input because the data previously installed has malfunctioned.

She knew Jesus loved Lazarus, but he had not come when they called. She knew he could have healed him, and the fact that he didn't come right away did not compute. She must have had the wrong data.

On his arrival, Jesus found that Lazarus had already been in the tomb for four days. Now Bethany was less than two miles from Jerusalem, and many Jews had come to Martha and Mary to comfort them in the loss of their brother. When Martha heard that Jesus was coming, she went out to meet him, but Mary stayed at home.

"Lord," Martha said to Jesus, "if you had been here, my brother would not have died. But I know that even now God will give you whatever you ask."

Jesus said to her, "Your brother will rise again."

Martha answered, "I know he will rise again in the resurrection at the last day."

Jesus said to her, "I am the resurrection and the life. The one who believes in me will live, even though they die; and whoever lives by believing in me will never die. Do you believe this?"

"Yes, Lord," she replied, "I believe that you are the Messiah, the Son of God, who is to come into the world."

After she had said this, she went back and called her sister Mary aside. "The Teacher is here," she said, "and is asking for you." . . .

Jesus, once more deeply moved, came to the tomb. It was a cave with a stone laid across the entrance. "Take away the stone," he said.

"But, Lord," said Martha, the sister of the dead man, "by this time there is a bad odor, for he has been there four days."

Then Jesus said, "Did I not tell you that if you believe, you will see the glory of God?" (John 11:17–28, 38–40)

In much the same way that Martha distorted the good works we are assigned as a part of our relationship with God, she also misunderstood the role that right belief plays in our life in God. As we did before, we must look at the end of the story in order to see beneath the surface of Martha's words.

Jesus said, "Did I not tell you that if you believe, you will see the glory of God?" (John 11:40)

"Did I not tell you?" Jesus had offered Martha an answer that she did not absorb. Though they had exchanged many words, there was no connection, no communication, no ability to hear or be heard, no transformation or healing. Though she confessed that she believed Jesus was the resurrection and the life, she was worried about the odor.

She confessed an orthodox belief; in fact, she practically quoted Peter's oft-admired confession, the rock upon which the church was founded. But her words seemed to be spoken for a different purpose than relating to Jesus. Perhaps she was seeking a kind of truth that was more knowable, predictable, and reliably certain than the flesh-and-blood disappointment of the God-man who stood before her. Her equation had not worked, so she was looking for a new one. She was desperate to believe that assent to a list of precepts would fix her life and end her pain. No matter how right, words and beliefs alone could not fill this hole in her hurting and confused heart, a hole undoubtedly larger than ever before.

The lack of recorded emotion from Martha is even more striking given the circumstance of her brother's death. For many of us, grief lowers our defenses and allows our vulnerable hearts to surface as we seek connection and the comfort therein. Yet Martha seems stuck in her safe place of knowing and certainty via theological understanding. Tragically, though the God of all comfort was standing right in front of her, she could not seem to find a way to let him in. Again, no matter how right her theology, without the accompanying relationship and connection with Christ, she remained empty.

Our final story seems to also convey the message that Martha did not hear what Jesus said to her in our first story.

Six days before the Passover, Jesus came to Bethany, where Lazarus lived, whom Jesus had raised from the dead. Here a dinner was given in Jesus' honor. Martha served, while Lazarus was among those reclining at the table with him. (John 12:1–2)

Once more, all we know of Martha is that she was serving. Again, there is nothing inherently wrong with serving; the kingdom of God is dependent upon it! But we cannot ignore the context that the other stories offer us when we read this one. We must at least consider the possibility that the record of her service here is meant to convey a continuance of the previously unhelpful pattern.

Superhuman as Inhumane

Martha is not unlike many of us. We try to mend our own hearts, broken in pieces by life, with one more Bible study or one more act of service. We confuse the choice to learn about God with the vulnerable and frightening challenge of experiencing him, of seeking his face, of opening our very souls to his real-time presence.

Like Martha, we focus energy on ever elusive attempts to "get our act together." We are fixated on our to-do lists and often live 90 percent of our waking moments multitasking, or as the descriptor goes, "distracted by all the preparations." Ironically, we are "worried and bothered" as we constantly prepare to live the life we never quite get around to actually living. We disallow our emotions, believing that if we go there we may never stop crying. We ignore the messages of our bodies. When we do stop long enough to catch our breath, we fall asleep. We become walking, talking human "doings."

As women in our modern world, we feel like our culture demands that we become superhuman. But the story of the people of God in Scripture is an amazingly human story. It is not superhuman, nor does it set before us a goal to rid ourselves of our emotions or our bodies to become more like machines. Yes, there are some miracles done by humans here and there, but by far it is a story of God at work in amazing ways in the midst of our unapologetically human reality with all its wonders, its foibles, and its limitations.

God does not relate to us as objects to be fixed. We are children who can both love and be loved. We are not computers to be programmed or machines meant for efficient production. We are gifted and talented women to be taught, received from, cherished, partnered with, pursued, comforted, and enjoyed.

My Story (continued)

Moving back into our former home, former church, and the schools our children had attended, I thought I would slip back into my old life seamlessly. But I did not. The island, or better, the God of the island, had changed me.

After two years without billboards, I felt as if every sign I passed on the highway was screaming at me to do this or buy that. I did not want to go to meetings or Bible studies or shopping. Suddenly such busyness and doing felt vacant and without meaning. I wanted my hands to be dirty again in my garden; something in me needed to handle the warm, moist soil, the earth itself. I wanted to plant and water and sit there and watch things grow. Though I still did not understand what was happening, I liked the woman I was becoming. I felt more alive than ever before.

About that time, I was reading a book on sexual abuse to help a teen in our church who was an abuse survivor. As the author described one of three different "self-protective relational styles," I suddenly saw a description of my way of life in print. Though I have no recollection of abuse, I had developed similar coping skills. I was struck to my core with unwelcome clarity and insight: All my utterly competent, duty-driven "doing good" was little more than a mask. Though undoubtedly God had used it to some extent, it was not the real me.

So who am I? The question was painful, startling, and even felt shameful. How could I get to age thirty-five with so little self-understanding? It was utterly humbling to be so clueless when I had seen myself as so competent and mature. The terror of my lack of self-understanding held a very real temptation for me. I wanted to slam the door on this deeply disturbing change, to sabotage this nascent work of God. Yet it was so clear to me that my way of being all these years was a sham that I could not bring myself to shut that door.

For thirty-five years that mask had worked; but now it was crumbling much faster than I could ever have imagined. Other than naked and afraid, I had no idea who I was.

Your *Story* ————————

1. Consider your answer to the opening question. Did anything in Martha's story or mine spark any new thoughts regarding your arenas of deadness?

2. Imagine someone saying to you, "Oh, you are such a woman." How do you imagine those words being spoken? How do you hear them? What is your response? Why do you think you imagined them in that way?

3. Are there aspects of your personhood that you use more than others as you engage in your relationship with God? Your intellect? Your body? Your emotions? Intuition? Are there some arenas that you generally don't bring to that relationship? How might you change that this week?

4. How do you generally regard your emotions—as friend or foe? Why?

5. Do you struggle with busyness? For the next five days, rate yourself in a miles-per-hour way at the end of the day. Is this the rate at which you want to live? Why or why not? What can you do this week to make any changes you feel God is moving you toward?

6. Is there a place in your life in which you or others are expecting you to be superhuman? Try to be specific

about why you feel that way. Have things been said, implied, or inferred? Have you taken on responsibilities from single conversations or have they accumulated over time? Are you meeting your own expectations or those of others? Do you think you meet God's expectations for your life? Prayerfully reexamine your thinking or talk through it with a wise friend.

7. What parts of your body are you most likely to treat as a machine to be used rather than human flesh to be honored, stewarded, and cared for? For example, you might eat too fast, regarding food only as fuel while forgetting to savor it and enjoy it as God intended. What will you do this week to be more humane to yourself?

MANY PHASES

4

Identity
Pretense vs. Presence

To be me

one of many voices
learning to stand tall
taking my whole space
no more no less
to be me
every moment
of
every day
with other voices
and
without

JANET DAVIS

CONSIDER: Make a list of ten words or phrases that describe the essence of you. Do not include roles you play, things you do, or

71

character qualities you have honed through the years. Do include qualities and characteristics that make you uniquely *you*: desires, preferences, gifts, values, passions.

My Story

Some of my earliest memories find me sitting barefoot and cross-legged under a large tree in our neighbor's backyard. My girlfriends and I were making purses out of large leaves, weaving the stiff stems through the fleshy edges. I enjoyed nature and creating beauty with my hands. I was a tender-hearted, very compliant, artistic little girl, who loved beauty from an early age.

Unfortunately, that gentle essence was pretty much out of line with the values in my immediate environment. I was raised in a part of the country whose entire economy was based on the exploitation of natural resources. Refinery fumes invaded our homes and non-air-conditioned schools as well as paid the bills. Our family culture valued important things like thrift, achievement, discipline, academic excellence, and faithfulness, but did not invest much in beauty, emotion, or the more tender aspects of life. There was little money for music lessons, ballet, frilly bedroom décor, store-bought clothes, or musical instruments. Makeup was discouraged; fashion was for others. Nor was there much interest in nature or travel.

Enriched by the family strengths and values present, I learned to be a very good student. Along the way, God provided manna for the more beauty-bent parts of me through neighbors and friends, books, art electives at school, youth group trips around the state, and teachers who encouraged me to write. But by and large, conscious awareness of that beauty-loving, tender part of my personal identity faded almost completely, going underground only to be resurrected at age thirty-five.

For many months, my new life (described in chapter 3) felt unsure and fragile. As the people in my world discovered that something was changing with me, I felt freer to adjust my schedule to better accommodate this massive internal shift. I resigned from virtually all of my ministry obligations and began to see a counselor every other week.

This was a season of intriguing and continual revelation. I spent several years becoming reacquainted with that little girl who loved to sit barefoot in the grass. I discovered that I am a gardener and an introvert. I found out that I am a deep thinker and that's just fine with God. In fact, it's a gift! I recovered my emotional sensitivity, and I learned that I have a large dose of the gift of mercy, a gift my made-to-be-a-corporate-executive thinking had denied completely.

Much of what I discovered had to do with my feminine identity. I began to wear makeup and became more aware of my emotional nature. I curled my hair and designed a new flower garden for our backyard. I became more aware within my relationships and let my deeply compassionate heart lead for a change. I felt both more pain and more joy with each day.

A good amount of the pain came from my struggles at church. As I grew and changed, I found myself with new questions, passions, and priorities. Right belief was now less important than a compassionate heart. *Being* mattered more to me than *doing*. Loving God and others meant more than getting the Christian life right. Though such distinctions may sound vague and small, they were not at all trivial at that point in my journey.

Noting both the dramatic change and my increasingly limited involvement, some in my church community were genuinely and understandably concerned for me. With these changes so new even to me, I had few words of consolation or explanation to offer. This was a group of people with whom I had shared years of my life and ministry. I loved them deeply and they loved me. Yet somehow, as I grew, the gap between us grew both wider and more painful. My husband and children experienced no such tension.

As I came to know my true self more and more, I began to possess such a sense of personal grounding and presence that my heart began to open to what God might be calling me to do in the kingdom at large. About that time, my husband and I attended a conference where the speaker was referencing the story of Moses. He highlighted how overtly God spoke of hearing the cry of his people when he called Moses. When he posed for us the question "Whose cry have you heard?" the response "wounded women in the church" surfaced immediately for me. Not long afterward, I realized that in order to do that work, I needed to continue my education in graduate school.

The decision to move our family for the sake of my education was a difficult one. The move would be a dream come true for me, more work for my husband, and genuine suffering for our kids, ages sixteen, thirteen, and ten. In that season of decision, the *Who do you think you are?* rant was almost everywhere I looked: friends, family, church, and within. But my sense of calling remained.

Just before we left, I directed a retreat for the women of our church, asking a counselor friend of mine to speak on "The Cry of a Woman's Heart." My role was to handle general administration, act as the emcee, and lead a gardening workshop. It was great fun to share some of the wisdom I had learned from God in my garden. The retreat felt like a lovely and appropriate parting gift to the community that had given me so very much through the years.

The move was costly and difficult, but oh so enlivening for me. I found myself, at age forty, in graduate school. Three thousand miles from my native homeland of Texas, I began to discover even more latent aspects of myself. I found that I love to listen. Previously, I thought my preference was to speak, to teach. Through feedback from others, I found out that I have a gentle presence. That surprised me. Though I knew I had changed internally from that hard, harsh person who actively fought against recognizing her tender, merciful heart, I had never realized that others could *see* that difference. My identity was becoming a reality on all fronts, one step at a time. What a transformation! I was also affirmed for my depth of thought and insight, a trait that, sadly and painfully, some had responded to by telling me I would be "of no use to God's kingdom" if I didn't think and speak more simply. I was willing and eager to accept and embrace these parts of my identity.

At the same time, when my professors affirmed my writing abilities, I was not willing to hear what they were saying, dismissing it as a pretense, a choice to be nice to me to keep me paying tuition! (I am now quite appalled and embarrassed by my cynicism! Self-contempt turned to contempt for others.) I also discovered that I was in the midst of a pendulum swing with regard to some of my self-perceptions. When I took a Myers-Briggs assessment in school that year, I scored near zero in *thinking* and near 100 percent in *feeling*. My academic record begged to differ. I needed time to settle into a more realistic sense of myself. As I noted in the introduction, this was also the season in my life when I began to become aware of my tendency toward self-sabotage.

These new self-discoveries began to subtly reshape my faith journey. I longed for stillness and silence, fewer words, more sacraments. With my barefoot-little-girl sensibilities restored, I needed to taste and touch and smell my worship. My faith shifted from being book- and knowledge-centered to becoming more gospel- and wisdom-centered. I was drawn to the perplexing and confounding teachings of Jesus. My merciful heart subtly shifted the priority from learning more about righteousness via books to receiving and offering more mercy via Communion and action. As one of my wise professors said, "You need a church with a different furniture arrangement." He was referencing the different emphases of traditions that place the pulpit front and center compared to those that are physically centered around an altar and Communion.

Graduate school was marvelous, but when our finances dictated an earlier than expected return a year later, I was struggling. Though I could complete my degree long-distance, I loved the Pacific Northwest. I did not want to move back to the refinery-filled landscape of southeast Texas. I knew I could not return to the same church. Even more sadly, I also knew that there was nothing I could say to those I loved that would adequately explain why.

The Syrophoenician Woman

Like many accounts of women in Scripture, this is a brief story. Brief, however, does not translate to small in meaning.

This text is much like the miracle sponge you see advertised on television: If we pour ourselves into it, we will see it expand before our eyes!

> *Jesus left that place and went to the vicinity of Tyre. He entered a house and did not want anyone to know it; yet he could not keep his presence secret. In fact, as soon as she heard about him, a woman whose little daughter was possessed by an impure spirit came and fell at his feet. The woman was a Greek, born in Syrian Phoenicia. She begged Jesus to drive the demon out of her daughter.*
>
> *"First let the children eat all they want," he told her, "for it is not right to take the children's bread and toss it to the dogs."*
>
> *"Lord," she replied, "even the dogs under the table eat the children's crumbs."*
>
> *Then he told her, "For such a reply, you may go; the demon has left your daughter."*
>
> *She went home and found her child lying on the bed, and the demon gone.* (Mark 7:24–30)

She Knew Who She Was

She was a woman. Not a man. She was a Greek. Not a Jew. She was born in Syrian Phoenicia. She was neither of the Promised Land nor one of Abraham's seed. She was a mother, perhaps a new mom, as the text says her daughter was little. She was in deep angst. Her daughter was possessed by a demon. She was a listener, possibly a friend of some local Jews. She heard of Jesus' arrival despite his desire to keep it secret.

She was bold. She went as soon as she heard. She was humble. She fell at his feet. She was desperate. She begged. She was singularly focused and she knew something of who

Jesus was. She asked this miracle-making rabbi for only one thing: to drive out the demon from her daughter. She knew who she was and she came as who she was. Not so hard, right?

Yesterday evening, I met with one of my spiritual direction clients who is about to get married. Because of some local scheduling conflicts, some old church politics, and an out-of-town location for the wedding, few of her church family are slated to attend. She expressed her deep hurt with many, many tears and very vocal anger. I had to fight to keep from smiling.

Don't misunderstand: I am not the least bit happy about my friend's pain. What made me want to smile was the fact that she came as who she was. She was fully present without pretense. She knew who she was and what she was feeling, and there was no gap between the internal identity and the external reality. For the last year since we have been meeting, most days she brought her brain but rarely her emotions or her body. Last evening, she was all there—a daring and vulnerable act of faith worthy of celebration (at another less painful moment). It is not a given that we always know who we are or approach others with bold and authentic relationship.

She Knew Who She Was Religiously and Culturally

The Syrophoenician woman was not clueless. She knew that when she came as she was, this Jewish rabbi would likely not even acknowledge her presence. Jews and Greeks (Gentiles) did not mix. It was socially and religiously forbidden, grounded in ancient custom and law. Wholesale rejection was the most likely course.

Perhaps she had heard of the compassion of this rabbi. Perhaps she was grasping with abandon at even the most remote straw. Perhaps the rejection would have simply echoed or validated what she was feeling from God as she watched her child suffer. She came knowing that it would take more than one miracle for her precious little one to be healed. First, she had to be heard.

Yet she came anyway. As herself. If that *Just who do you think you are?* accusation had been raised within her, she would have simply and confidently answered it. She did not try to create a more acceptable identity or obtain a proxy, perhaps a Jewish friend who might plead her case. There was no pretense, only a willingness to be fully and honestly present. This was indeed a choice of great faith.

She Knew a Deeper Truth

This story really opens up when we consider the context. Just before this encounter, Jesus had a moment of frustration with his disciples. The question at hand was "What makes a person acceptable (clean)?" Surprisingly, Jesus' teaching was that it had nothing to do with the external. In verses 1–14, just before our story, the Pharisees had initiated the conversation with talk of ceremonial washing before meals. Jesus expanded the conversation with an Isaiah reference: *"These people honor me with their lips, but their hearts are far from me"* (Mark 7:6). He also mentioned issues way too close to home for them, such as how poorly they were treating their parents. He concluded with remarks about evil being inside out, not outside in.

> *Again Jesus called the crowd to him and said, "Listen to me, everyone, and understand this. Nothing outside a person can defile them by going into them. Rather, it is what comes out of a person that defiles them."*

> *After he had left the crowd and entered the house, his disciples asked him about this parable. "Are you so dull?" he asked. "Don't you see that nothing that enters a person from the outside can defile them? For it doesn't go into their heart but into their stomach, and then out of the body." (In saying this, Jesus declared all foods clean.)*
>
> *He went on: "What comes out of a person is what defiles them. For it is from within, out of a person's heart, that evil thoughts come—sexual immorality, theft, murder, adultery, greed, malice, deceit, lewdness, envy, slander, arrogance and folly. All these evils come from inside and defile a person."* (Mark 7:14–23)

I don't believe this story was placed just after this teaching by accident. This deeper understanding of clean and unclean was the very truth this unnamed woman from Syrian Phoenicia not only knew intuitively, but was also banking on big time.

She Sensed the Source of Power and Hoped for Mercy

Scripture is full of non-Jewish women who saw and sought the power and mercy of the God of the Jews. Think of Rahab, who had heard the rumors of what God had done for his nation and declared her belief to the spies (Joshua 2). She knew where the power was, and she approached, seeking mercy. Think of Ruth, the Moabite. Undoubtedly expecting rejection based on her nationality, she followed her Jewish mother-in-law Naomi back to Naomi's homeland. Ruth, too, knew where the power was, and she approached, seeking mercy. And mercy she received through her loyal and kind choices, her creative mother-in-law, Naomi, the provision of the law, and the faithfulness of her kinsman redeemer Boaz (Ruth 1–4).

My guess is that each of these three women knew more through their feminine intuition and relational sensitivities than through rational, theological, or analytical knowing. They were not "dull" like Jesus' disciples. They sensed in their innermost being that this was the direction of salvation and life, and then followed the Spirit's prompting.

She Planted Herself and Persisted in What She Knew

I have heard lots of defenses for Jesus' remark to her, but still it never fails to impact me like a slap in the face. Some say the word he uses for *dog* is a reference to a valued pet. That's not much comfort. What has been helpful, though, is to read the whole of this story through the lens of the end of the narrative. The telling conclusion finds Jesus healing the daughter and affirming the woman's reply as the reason for that healing.

With that lens in place, I read her response not as agreeing to a contemptuous label, but as standing tall and courageously in the presence of harsh religious and cultural realities. " *'Lord,' she replied, 'even the dogs under the table eat the children's crumbs' "* (Mark 7:28). What a brilliant, shining retort. This spirited woman grounded herself in the reality of who she was—in the midst of an overtly acknowledged social/religious context that devalued her—and asked anyway. It is as if she were saying, "Yes. I know who I am and who I am not. I know that I have no externally based right to be here asking for a miracle. I also know I am a mother with a sick child. A sick child whom I have heard you can heal. I know it and I believe it. Crumbs? Hey, I'll take them. No problem."

This wise and astonishingly brave woman stood her ground. There were logical reasons for rejection. Yet she was completely authentic and unwaveringly unapologetic. Listening with her eyes and her heart, how could she have missed or doubted the mercy in Jesus' eyes? Something in her knew that logic and laws, nationality and status, the externals Jesus had just devalued in his teaching with his disciples, are never the greatest reality. She knew the very thing that the disciples could not grasp. The fact that she so boldly evidenced this knowing, this heart-based, internally defined holiness might well be the larger message of this side-by-side section of Scripture.

Crumbs Are Enough

I see within this story a duality to the "crumbs are enough" message. We often believe that the reality of who we are is not enough. We are not loving enough, smart enough, caring enough, tough enough, beautiful enough, and on and on. So we pretend to be someone or something else. I call it the *Wizard of Oz* syndrome. Poor Oz, he was hidden behind that curtain, feeling like he was only enough in the pretense of Oz the Great and Terrible. He saw his limited human presence as a crumb. What he didn't realize was that when we are crumbs fallen from the Master's table, we are enough.

A huge part of the Syrophoenician woman's faith was the fact that she came to Jesus as a fragile and limited human being. No pretense or manipulation, no screen or great and terrible image—she was a needy and real woman. Just as she believed that the crumbs from Israel's table could heal her daughter, she also believed that the crumb of who she was would be enough to be heard.

Jesus Honored Her

For such a reply, you may go; the demon has left your daughter. (v. 29).

Jesus tied her daughter's healing directly to this Gentile woman's brilliant and shining retort. He did not miss her courage and he rewarded her faith. She had persisted in both the reality of the limitations of who she was and in her desire for and expectation of mercy. She walked into the house likely expecting rejection, but she refused the temptation to talk herself out of going or to run away. Neither did she compromise, deny, enhance, or hide her identity.

My Story (continued)

In August 1998, we moved back to Beaumont. I had found such life in my graduate school community; amazingly deep connections formed in a single year of shared learning, now torn asunder. As our family returned, I leaned into instead of away from my sadness for the first time. The only thing I knew was that God had not brought me back to die. I could hardly stand to be inside and spent most of that first fall working in my yard. I transplanted grass in September heat and tearfully planted a dozen encore azaleas in forty-degree misting rain on Christmas Eve.

Alongside the grief were some amazing surprises, seeds of new life God was planting in the loose, tear-moist soil of my life. We began attending a local Episcopal church. I felt as if I were finally home. This tradition suited my newly recovered identity perfectly. I found life and new avenues for growth in this ancient tradition that emphasized the Gospels in teaching and weekly Communion in worship. I also located a spiritual director, an ancient discipline I had learned about in school, and began meeting with her monthly.

Over time, with my spirit so well fed, I gave back to my church community through leading a grief group at the request of our pastor. I loved the work and was genuinely helpful to others. It suited my listening and emotional sensibilities and my depth of thought. I also created and offered a workshop for women, "Women, Wisdom, and the Word," exploring how one might nurture feminine spirituality through the interplay of Scripture, creativity, and small-group conversation. For the first time, I felt as if my ministry and my giftedness, my work and my identity, were well matched, hand in glove. I was letting my light shine, fully present without the need for pretense, operating on all cylinders. When I confronted that core, accusing question of self-sabotage *Just who do you think you are?* I actually had an answer! What a difference that made in both my efficacy and my satisfaction.

My next adventure was an unexpected one: hospital chaplaincy. With our first child's pending departure for college, my husband and I knew that more income was needed. I was actually interviewing for a different position when Sister Margaret Mary offered me a job as a chaplain. She was a wise and intuitive woman who reminded me over and over, "Do the job as only you can do it. Listen to yourself as a woman and follow that path." Though there were some rough days at first, soon, with Sister Margaret Mary's steady encouragement and positive feedback from within and without, I found chaplaincy to be both a place of effective ministry and an opportunity to stretch and strengthen my capacity for service. I was daring to shine as a gentle, listening healer.

Nevertheless, I would soon discover that chaplaincy wouldn't necessarily be my only kingdom contribution.

Your *Story*

1. Review your list of identity descriptors. How do you feel about each one? Are there some you like better than others and some you don't like at all?

2. Now make a list of five identities, traits, or gifts you definitely do not possess, but may wish you did or think you should. For each one, ask: How often do I find myself apologizing for this limitation? Have I experienced rejection because of this limitation? When? Tell the story.

3. For each trait/non-trait, briefly reflect on how you came to recognize that identity. Which are newer discoveries? Which are older?

4. Can you identify moments or seasons of pretense in your life, past or ongoing? What traits did you deny? Take on? What has been the fruit of those choices?

5. What kind of value do you place on each trait? Are there some that you particularly devalue? How would/do your parents feel about or value that trait/non-trait? What about your faith community?

6. Where in your life do you find affirmation/acceptance for each trait/non-trait? Where is there resistance or even shame? Read the verse below.

> *The Lord your God is with you, he is mighty to save.*
> *He will take great delight in you, he will quiet you*

*with his love, he will rejoice over you with singing.
(Zephaniah 3:17)*

Do you have a sense of God singing over that part of who you are?

7. Is the life you are currently living—including your faith tradition, job, ministry, recreational choices, and time priorities—in sync with your core identity or in tension with it?

5

Creativity

Conformity vs. Uniqueness

What Is Prayer?

. . . So be awake to the life that is loving you
and sing your prayer, laugh your prayer,
dance your prayer, run
and weep and sweat your prayer,
sleep your prayer, eat your prayer,
paint, sculpt, hammer and read your prayer,
sweep, dig, rake, drive and hoe your prayer,
garden and farm and build and clean your prayer,
wash, iron, vacuum, sew, embroider and pickle
  your prayer,
compute, touch, bend and fold, but never delete
or mutilate your prayer.

Learn and play your prayer,
work and rest your prayer,
fast and feast your prayer,
argue, talk, whisper, listen and shout your prayer,
groan and moan and spit and sneeze your prayer,

swim and hunt and cook your prayer,
digest and become your prayer.

Release and recover your prayer.
Breathe your prayer.
Be your prayer. . . .[1]

ALLA RENÉE BOZARTH

CONSIDER: What is your favorite creative medium? Think far beyond the arts as traditionally defined. You might prefer creating holiday meals, curriculum, a garden, a logical argument, an organizational structure, research hypotheses, travel itineraries, child discipline approaches, or shopping strategies. Remember: Made in the image of our creative Creator, you are creative by design.

My Story

From my first days as a chaplain, I considered the work to be a holy and rare privilege. Connecting with people in their most physically vulnerable moments with defenses stripped away by suffering and hearts opened by pain was a sacred responsibility. I also discovered that the pace was absolutely exhausting.

Accustomed to being home alone most of the day for ten years, I was now meeting fifty-plus new people a day. It was not so much the depth of the work but the breadth that wore on me: too many faces; too many moments to digest. I could feel my soul stretching. In part, that seemed good; my capacity needed some increase, my introverted soul needed to be challenged.

But as months became years, I was wearing down quickly. With our most costly years of college expenses behind us, my husband and I began to consider the possibility of my working part time, in part due to my fatigue, but also because of my desire to write.

My journey as a writer began at age seventeen. My English teacher asked me to compete in a writing competition. Believe it or not, it never occurred to me that she asked me because she thought I could write well! As mentioned previously, my graduate school professors also commented on my writing. Like water off a duck's back, their words did not penetrate. Nevertheless, quite apart from acknowledging any giftedness, I had an intuitive sense that I had something to write. For years, I had collected thoughts and personal reflections on the stories of women in Scripture that had proven healing for me. At a deep level, I knew that there was a book in me that needed to be born.

Though the calling to write seemed vague, the voices of opposition were much clearer. Each time an inspiring thought began to flicker into flame, convincing internal objections would arise. *Who do you think you are? You have no experience. No one in your family has ever written anything. Writing is not even on your radar screen of possibilities. That's for others who are better and smarter than you. And you have no connections, anyway. You could never get published.* Or I would step into a bookstore and rather than the collective mass of books telling me "We did it; so can you!" my internal censor would sound: *Just look at all these books! Who needs another one? It has all been said and done. Don't bother. How could you possibly have anything new to say?* The objections were fierce.

Yet as our family moved back to Texas after graduate school, a friend and I teamed up and made a decision to write a book together. But living in different states, having different lives and different work habits, it did not take long to know it just wasn't going to work. Though that initial attempt was a bust, somehow the process affirmed my sense that I really did have something to say. I also learned that I was all too quick to abandon my voice and defer to a co-author. My willingness to hold on to my own thoughts and perspective was so fragile that I knew I had to do this alone. At the time of those realizations, however, life interrupted. The book ideas went in a drawer, and I accepted the previously mentioned job as a hospital chaplain, hoping to pick up the project after adjusting to the hospital work.

I soon discovered that was harder than I imagined it might be. The only writing I could manage during my first few years at the job was to pen a few stories about my chaplaincy work for a corporate publication called *Miracle Moments*. As my husband and I continued to discuss the possibility of my working part time, I was surprised to discover that my full-time position at the hospital was very difficult to release. I had built trusting and good relationships with many of the staff; we were a team. The work was predictably meaningful. The comfort I offered others was real, and I was making a definite, daily difference in the kingdom. Patients, family, staff, and peers gave me very positive and very frequent feedback as to my effectiveness. There was never a shortage of new people in pain. If I was not there, who would be with them? With several unfilled positions in our department, chaplains were in short supply.

With the needs so apparent, and my deep love of the essence of the work so real, it was all too easy to deny my personal pain and exhaustion. I had spent forty years writing myself out of consideration in moments like this. A big part of my struggle was the idea of faithfulness. I had always defined it in simplistic terms of service to God through service to others. To acknowledge my human limitations and exhaustion, my preferences, and other less predictably fruitful passions like writing seemed frivolous and unfaithful. More than once I said to myself, *Come on, now, muscle through this. Your life is one of service and sacrifice. This is not complicated. God gave you this job. Life is not supposed to be easy or fun. It's the narrow way, not the fun way. Just who do you think you are?* The pastoral care needs of others became a tyrant within my mind as much as a holy opportunity. My effectiveness at the job became evidence to use against my passion and intuition and growing self-awareness. My exhaustion became shameful weakness, not simple human limitation.

Nevertheless, amazingly, I began to make slow progress toward putting my thoughts on paper. A wise woman once told me to listen most closely to the things you cannot *not* do: there you will find your passion and your gift. Writing was clearly something I could not *not* do. Through many months of struggle, I began to recognize writing as a genuine calling, not simply as a persistent vague intuition or interest. The unlikelihood that the work would be published ceased to be an effective excuse; I was convinced that my thoughts at least needed to be written. My boss consented to a part-time schedule, and I began to write.

Mary of Bethany

Mary of Bethany is directly connected to three different gospel stories: sitting at Jesus' feet to listen, falling at Jesus' feet after her brother Lazarus died, and anointing Jesus' feet, likely just before his death. Though, as we noted in chapter 3, we cannot be certain about the time sequence of these events, we made some reasonable assumptions and will do the same as we engage Mary's story. As with Martha, we will listen to these stories of Mary of Bethany collectively, as a single story of growth progression.

We will also be looking at Mary's story through the lens of the creative process. The last of the three stories, Mary's anointing of Jesus, was a beautiful expression of her creativity. As we listen to the first two stories, we will highlight the essential elements common to creativity, the soil and seeds that eventually form good fruit.

Cultivating Fertile Ground

As Jesus and his disciples were on their way, he came to a village where a woman named Martha opened her home to him. She had a sister called Mary, who sat at the Lord's feet listening to what he said. But Martha was distracted by all the preparations that had to be made. She came to him and asked, "Lord, don't you care that my sister has left me to do the work by myself? Tell her to help me!"

"Martha, Martha," the Lord answered, "you are worried and upset about many things, but few things are needed—or indeed only one. Mary has chosen what is better, and it will not be taken away from her." (Luke 10:38–42)

For many of us, this is a very familiar story . . . familiar to the point that it is very difficult to see new messages in the well-known text. With Martha's struggle being the larger part of this narrative and the most common emphasis, we may not have thought much about Mary.

The text doesn't say a lot about her. She utters no words. All we know is that Mary chose not to help Martha, creating a tension in that relationship, and sat at Jesus' feet listening. So what can we see in those two choices?

First, it appears that this was a new choice for Mary: Martha was accustomed to her help. It is easy to underestimate the impact of small choices, but leaving well-worn behavioral ruts is not a small thing. It is especially bold and challenging when that leaving causes those we love some sense of pain and loss. The creative process often begins as the hard ground and packed dirt of life's routines become loose soil, broken up by such small but critically important "rut-busting" choices.

Second, we know culturally that Mary's choice to sit at Jesus' feet was a radical move for a woman. She was breaking the rules: Men were allowed and encouraged to sit with rabbis to learn; women were not. But Jesus supported Mary's choice. Such rule-breaking decisions are also often an essential part of the necessary ground breaking.

Third, let's look at what is not here: There are no words from Mary, no movement whatsoever. She is still and silent. Often we underestimate the importance of negative or empty space within the creative process. Since creativity is such a spiritual dynamic—a partnership with God sprouting from our made-in-the-image-of-God soul—it stands to reason that a listening posture of silence and stillness is commonly an essential component.

Shared Pain as the Seed of Creative Passion

Our first Mary story could be seen as speaking to the rut-busting soil preparation for a new work of God. In like manner, we can see this second Mary story as the planting of seeds—seeds of compassion that in time grow into passionate ministry toward others. This is the story of the death and resurrection of Lazarus. We pick up Mary's part of the story at the end of Jesus' conversation with Martha. (If you need more context, the whole story is found in John 11:1–44.)

> After [Martha] had said this, she went back and called her sister Mary aside. "The Teacher is here," she said, "and is asking for you." When Mary heard this, she got up quickly and went to him. . . .
>
> When Mary reached the place where Jesus was and saw him, she fell at his feet and said, "Lord, if you had been here, my brother would not have died."
>
> When Jesus saw her weeping, and the Jews who had come along with her also weeping, he was deeply moved in spirit and troubled. "Where have you laid him?" he asked.
>
> "Come and see, Lord," they replied.
>
> Jesus wept.
>
> Then the Jews said, "See how he loved him!"
>
> But some of them said, "Could not he who opened the eyes of the blind man have kept this man from dying?" (John 11:28–29, 32–37)

In this second story, we hear Mary's voice for the first and only time in all three narratives: *"Lord, if you had been here, my brother would not have died."* Spoken in the context of weeping at Jesus' feet, these words give voice to her enormous anguish. Though technically a statement of great faith, assuming Jesus' absolute healing power, these words also voice the unspoken questions "Why, oh why, were you not here?" "Why did you let this happen?" "Why did you not heal this one I know you loved so much?"

Jesus saw and shared Mary's pain: *"He was deeply moved in spirit and troubled"* and *"Jesus wept."* Notice that he did not offer explanations or excuses. Instead, he offered himself, his passion and emotion, his heart. He met her in her agony and the two hearts began to beat and hurt together. Then and only then did he move to the tomb.

Jesus' encounter with Martha (vv. 17–27) had a much different feel: there was no emotion, no movement, only words. I sense little relational connection in the story of her encounter with Jesus. Could our first Mary story speak to this difference? Could it be that Mary's choice to sit at Jesus' feet and listen created a much stronger and more intimate relationship with him, such that in this unforeseen moment of pain and crisis, Mary had access to both greater comfort and deeper faith?

Think about how this story might have been different. Jesus could well have gone directly to the tomb and brought Lazarus back to life immediately. He could have avoided this grief scene altogether. What was it that made this moment so essential? What did such shared pain accomplish? Though the text tells us twice that this whole scenario was intended to help people believe (vv. 15, 42), I still struggle.

Once again, though, I see new meaning here when I connect this story to the next. Could it be that the passion and connection in the midst of confusion and grief were the seeds of inspiration for Mary's creative expression of love that follows one chapter later in John's gospel? Could it be that because Jesus met her in her pain, she could not only see his anguish as he neared death, but she also brought all she had and all she was to creatively comfort this one she loved so much?

Bringing Her All and Her Best

Six days before the Passover, Jesus came to Bethany, where Lazarus lived, whom Jesus had raised from the dead. Here a dinner was given in Jesus' honor. Martha served, while Lazarus was among those reclining at the table with him. Then Mary took about a pint of pure nard, an expensive perfume; she poured it on Jesus' feet and wiped his feet with her hair. And the house was filled with the fragrance of the perfume.

But one of his disciples, Judas Iscariot, who was later to betray him, objected, "Why wasn't this perfume sold and the money given to the poor? It was worth a year's wages." He did not say this because he cared about the poor but because he was a thief; as keeper of the money bag, he used to help himself to what was put into it.

"Leave her alone," Jesus replied. "It was intended that she should save this perfume for the day of my burial. You will always have the poor among you, but you will not always have me." (John 12:1–8)

Notice that once again, for a third time, Mary is at Jesus' feet. This time she brought pure nard. As you may know, nard was a very valuable and concentrated perfume, and many people of the day used it as security for the future. Here Mary poured it out with enough generosity that the fragrance filled the room. The writer tells us it was a pint, worth a year's wages. She brought her best.

I love the detail that she wiped his feet with her hair. The image in my mind is almost so intimate that I want to turn away. Not many years later, the apostle Paul offers a cultural perspective on a woman's hair, referring to it as her glory (1 Corinthians 11:15). Mary was fully invested in this offering of faith and comfort: body, soul, and spirit. She brought her best and her all to this expression of deep love. She connected with Jesus in his humanity, his suffering, and his grief.

Her Suffering Opened Her Eyes to His

We all have a strong tendency to see only what we know, what we are expecting to see. We tend to focus our vision according to past experiences. Though we could interpret that limitation as a blindness, which it is, the other side of that coin is that our past experiences tune our vision to see and connect with others in the midst of similar life moments.

Perhaps that is why Mary could see Jesus' grief in these last few days before his death. It certainly seems that his disciples missed it, with all their talk of who would be the right-hand man. Mary knew deep grief; she even shared it with Jesus. She saw his face in that moment of being deeply troubled and weeping. She knew what such anguish of soul looked like, tasted like, and smelled like. She also knew the comfort that is possible when someone you love willingly shares your tears.

Too Much Message for Words Alone

As with the death of Lazarus, Mary likely saw the possibility of Jesus' death as one of those events that simply should not be happening. Martha's first words to Jesus after Lazarus' death were identical to Mary's, offering us an emphasis that draws our attention: *"Lord, if you had been here, my brother would not have died."* Both women were experiencing what psychologists call cognitive dissonance. That is, they were facing the reality of two truths that seemed like they could not coexist: Jesus was the healing rabbi who loved Lazarus, and Jesus did not come in time to heal him.

Experiences of cognitive dissonance feel like crazy-making moments. Either they stretch our brains and our categories, or we punt and move toward either/or thinking, sacrificing one truth or the other. At the tomb, Martha was caught in established thinking, worried about the smell. Mary chose the more difficult way: She engaged both realities and opened herself to a larger truth.

This moment in Jesus' life had the same quality of dissonance for Mary. She knew two things: Jesus was the anointed one of God, the Messiah, and Jesus was deeply grieved because he was going to die soon. Those two facts did not go together. They appeared to be mutually exclusive. Yet because of Mary's unique story, her previous life experience, she not only held them both as true, she brilliantly crafted an experience that could hold both seemingly irreconcilable truths at once, letting Jesus know that he was not alone.

Think about it. She anointed Jesus, communicating, "You are the Messiah, the anointed one of God." *With the same action,* she anointed him with oil for his burial (v. 7), implying, "Your death is near." Her previous painful life experience became her deep wisdom and the seed of phenomenal inspiration for her creative soul, which she now used to bless and comfort Jesus. Her story shaped her ministry; her identity shaped her creativity.

Internal Authority as Maturity

Judas, and likely all the disciples, did not see the depth of what was unfolding before their eyes in these days just before Jesus' death. Mary did. Even more important, she did not let the fact that she *alone* saw this reality cause her to doubt her perception or diminish her creative offering.

Any time we create, we take a risk. Think about the subtle (or stark) terror many of us feel when we sit before a blank sheet of paper. Creativity asks us to find within ourselves an internal authority, a God-validated voice that has a message like none other. The challenge is that a truly creative act is by definition something that reflects our unique soul; and as such, it is something that requires that we stand both exposed and alone. Exposed and alone is not a posture for the weak or faint at heart.

So sadly, many of us punt. In genuine fear, we shield ourselves from such vulnerability through self-doubt. We regress to nightmarish junior-high-art-class feelings of panic. We are convinced there's nothing unique or of worth inside us that could possibility be revealed on the page. Or if we do dare to create, we desperately hide our handiwork from those around us. Lacking the wisdom or courage for internal authority, we compare and contrast ourselves to others. We peek at our neighbor's work. We play to the crowd, echoing things others have done or said.

Tragically, we choose to secure our belonging through conformity and compliance rather than daring authenticity, diversity, and trust. We sabotage our creativity. That which had such divinely imagined potential for shining with brilliant goodness and beauty is twisted into something ordinary or common.

Beauty and Goodness

Mary chose differently. She risked standing exposed and alone so that Jesus would feel less alone in his suffering. Her courageous choice raises some uncomfortable questions for us. For instance, she chose to act on what she alone could see. So why do we wait for others to see it our way before we act? She created a moment that held a difficult message larger than words could contain. So why do we feel that we need to be able to explain our intuition or fit the entire vision on a line before we take the first step? Mary chose to give all that she was and all that she had. What a way to shine!

My Story (continued)

Working only two days a week, I completed the first few chapters of the manuscript. I was pleasantly surprised to notice how much my chaplaincy work had become a part of what I was writing. Though I had not been aware of the process, I had been gathering within myself some great examples for the work ahead.

Through such a small beginning, my sense of identity and calling as a writer was increasing and broadening. I became the resident wordsmith for two different committees on which I served. For the first time, I didn't run from that label. With the helpful feedback of others, I also began to trust my perspective on the stories of women in Scripture as unique. For the very first time, I started to believe that maybe, just maybe, the world did need another book. Maybe I did have a healing perspective to share, or at least attempt to share. (Being published still appeared highly unlikely.)

I began to confront my fears one at a time: the fear of facing critics, of being forever wrong in print, of disappointing others. As I dealt with each fear, I found the act of grounding myself in the reality of who I was and who I was not to be the most helpful approach. The best response to my *Just who do you think you are?* internal rant was a direct answer. "I am ____; I am not ____," factually, unapologetically, and without shame for my human limitations. Knowing my struggle, a dear friend made a brightly colored small clay figure, a palm-size sphere with tiny ankles and adorable feet and the word *ENOUGH* written across her ball-shaped form. "Miss Enough" lived on my desk.

As I made progress, I sought to market the proposal to several publishing companies without success. I knew that even part-time chaplaincy was a huge energy drain and slowing my work. Yet I could not bring myself to leave that holy and satisfying job altogether. So God made the decision for me. A month later, my part-time chaplaincy job ended. Sister Margaret Mary had taken a new assignment and our new department director did not believe in part-time chaplains. *Poof!* My job was gone. Interestingly, on my last day at the hospital, the corporate website, clearly unaware of that fact, featured one of the *Miracle Moments* articles I had written front and center. What an utterly gracious segue!

Several months later, once the manuscript was complete and roughly edited, I crafted an email to a developmental editor who had politely turned me down the previous year. It was an honest rendition of why I felt their company needed to publish this book. I respectfully asked if she would reconsider. To my amazement, she was willing.

The multiple committee process that had taken months before took only weeks now. The final committee was to meet Friday. That morning, I knew I could not wait around in the house all day. As was my custom, I went to the eleven-thirty mass at a local monastery. I arrived early and as I was sitting in the quiet, I realized (to my amusement) that I was trying to "pump" God for the answer. Would it be yes, or would they say no? I was seeking to tune myself to God in prayer to see if he might leak an intuitive hint, just so I would be prepared. No hints came.

However, I did have an interesting impression as the service continued. I heard (without hearing), "Whatever the response, you are ready. You have what it takes to move forward." I did not realize until that moment of reassurance that I was more afraid of a yes than a no! A no only required more perseverance: been there, done that. I had no idea what a yes would ask of me. I came home to a blinking message machine and the congratulations of an enthusiastic and excited editor! My journey of creativity, with all its twists, turns, and challenges, was transitioning into a journey of shining.

Your *Story*

1. Review your list of favorite media for creativity. Write or tell a friend one story of when you enjoyed creating. Try to record any internal experiences you recall: thoughts, feelings, temptations, or fears. Notice any emotion that arises in you as you tell/write the story.

2. Can you think of a time when stillness or silence increased your creativity and inspired new ideas?

3. Scripture says that we comfort with the comfort we ourselves have received from God (2 Corinthians 1:3–4). Tell a story of a moment when your own experience of pain and comfort was the seed of inspiration for the creative comfort you offered another. Again, think of creativity in a broad sense.

4. Can you recall a time when you compromised your creative vision for fear of rejection? When you elected to play to the crowd?

5. What is the most creative thing you did this week? Even very small rut-busting choices count!

6. Name the people in your life from whom you hide your creative soul. Journal about any particular experiences with each that might have informed that decision.

7. Name the people in your life with whom you are most free to be creative. Explore those relationships more specifically. What makes them feel safe? Are you safe to reveal your most creative parts to *yourself*? How do you generally respond to your creative self?

8. On a scale of 1–10 with 10 being a large amount, rate your personal sense of inner authority, that conviction that you, in partnership with God, have a unique and important message or creative offering for the kingdom of God.

6

Shining

Recoiling vs. Radiance

The jump
    is so frightening
       between
where i am and
    where i want to be . . .
because of all
    i may become
i will close my eyes
    and leap![1]

MARY ANNE RADMACHER

CONSIDER: Describe a moment in which you observed someone shining. What gave them that quality? What did you observe about them that led to your perception of radiance? What was the context of that moment for them? What came before or just after?

My Story

When I was a girl, I absolutely loved the Rodgers and Hammerstein version of *Cinderella*. I knew the lyrics to every song Lesley Ann Warren sang and fought with my brothers and father every year it came on, always, it seemed, opposite some "once in a lifetime" sporting event. (Remember: I grew up in the era when most families owned a *single* black-and-white TV set!) So if you had asked me then what my image of shining would look like, I would have undoubtedly described Cinderella at the ball . . . floating across the dance floor, admired by all (save her stepmother and stepsisters), in control of the moment, and safely in the arms of a powerful and loving prince. Idyllic perfection.

My expectations of shining as a published author were not far from that image. God had opened this miraculous door, and I expected nothing but smooth sailing to follow. I soon discovered, however, that my fairy-tale-rooted expectations weren't realistic, or very biblical! You can imagine my shock and multilevel disillusionment when in the same week that I signed my first book contract we also discovered that our twenty-three-year-old, one-week-into-law-school son, Bobby, had a tumor in the middle of his brain. Thus began my free fall into reality and my redefinition of shining.

Two of the biggest moments in my life were happening at the same time, each on an opposite end of the emotional spectrum. I felt like I needed lizard eyes, one fixed on one end of the continuum and the other turned in the opposite direction, to take it all in. My soul was being stretched more than I knew possible. How could I *not* celebrate my first book deal? In this context, how *could* I celebrate? I even offered the contract up as a sacrificial lamb, just in case God was in

a mood to bargain. No such luck. Suddenly the disappointment of a distant release date for the book (eighteen months)
was divine provision.

In the confused mix of those days, I encountered Isaiah
60:1, *"Arise, shine, for your light has come, and the glory of
the Lord rises upon you."* Reading that verse one morning, I
noticed an unexpected response: a deep sense of terror. It was
announcing good news. Why did it scare me? Within days,
our daughter Jenna shared a poem with me that referenced
growth as ever-widening circles. Another terrifying thought.

Widening circles? Shining? No thank you. Home: that's
where I wanted to be. All I desired was to crawl up in my
bed and pull the covers over my head until the tumor went
away. Until I knew everything would be fine, I would just
absent myself from dealing with the world, book deal or no
book deal. With gentle persistence, God was moving me in
the opposite direction.

We began to schedule doctor visits as soon as possible. I
matched each bit of new information with countless hours
of Internet research. Thankfully, we could tell from initial
testing that the tumor was slow-growing, albeit in a bad spot.
Miraculously, it had almost surrounded our son's optic nerve
junction without harming his vision. Talking to a range of
doctors from coast to coast, we were offered an equally wide
range of opinions. Some saw the tumor as inoperable, with
surgery doing more harm than good. Others felt they would
attempt to get it all surgically. Still others advised us to wait
and do nothing until we were forced into action by worsening
symptoms. That December, Bobby had a biopsy (no small
thing) that confirmed the tumor as potentially responsive to
radiation, offering us yet another treatment possibility.

During that autumn of doctor visits, Bobby decided to defer his law school education and moved home in October. That same month, I received an invitation from an organization to give a workshop on the content of my book at their national conference in California the following February. What an opportunity! How could I *not* go? But then again, how *could* I go?

As winter set in, I was still struggling with that decision at a level far more profound than simple time and money management. I felt conflicted about my identity. Does being a faithful mom preclude my leaving home at such a time as this? My new author identity seemed oh so easy to dismiss. Yet the trip also represented a once-in-a-lifetime opportunity to offer this wonderfully healing message of God to a broader audience. The calendar said I could do both; my heart was not so sure.

As the deadline for the conference opportunity approached, we made a final decision on the tumor treatment, opting for two months of proton beam radiation in Boston. Boston? California? Talk about living my life in "widening circles". . . literally! God was not accommodating my fearful heart, which was still seeking the comfort of narrow and familiar spaces.

A few months earlier I had had a dream that I recorded. I was in a large room, filled with soft yellow sunlight. The creamy, sun-yellowed walls and the golden wood floors beautifully reflected the light that streamed in from a two-story wall of multi-paned windows. The room was empty except for me. I was dancing with great grace and freedom, inspired by and thoroughly enjoying the large open space. As I awoke, the images of that dream stayed with me as did the clear message: Big rooms are made for dancing. Though I did not understand the dream, I somehow felt I needed to hold on to that image.

That dream came back to me as I struggled over buying that plane ticket to California. Big rooms did not have to be frightening, they could be inspiring and enjoyable; they could be spaces filled with dancing. I bought my ticket to California. As my coast-to-coast plans progressed, a dear friend's daughter who lived near Boston found the perfect place for us in the city. Though she had no prior knowledge of my dream, the condo she found had a living area with soft yellow walls, one with two stories of large multi-paned windows, and gleaming hardwood floors. Though this story of shining was not playing out anything like I had imagined, and it was full of external and internal challenges, all I could think was, *"Arise, shine, for your light has come, and the glory of the Lord rises upon you."*

Esther

The story of Esther is a wild tale full of complexity, humor, courage, and intrigue. It is a particularly dramatic story of God's protection of the Jewish people while they were in exile.

Saying Yes to Giftedness and Opportunity

Mordecai had reared his cousin Hadassah, otherwise known as Esther, since she had no father or mother. The girl had a good figure and a beautiful face. After her parents died, Mordecai had adopted her. (Esther 2:7 THE MESSAGE)

We are first introduced to Esther as a woman gifted with beauty of both figure and face. When we read such a description within the context of our modern culture, many of us wince. Tragically, the world around us has taken the gift of feminine beauty and airbrushed it into a destructive tool often used to objectify and devalue women. Sadly, in a reactionary posture, the church has often swung the pendulum so far in the opposite direction that many women fear their God-given beauty and even see it as a liability to their spiritual journey.

I invite you to consider Esther's beauty apart from our cultural baggage. Beauty, like any other inborn trait, is a gift, but it also requires stewardship. As gift, we are invited to enjoyment, gratitude, and appreciation. As stewardship, we are called to recognize and use such an endowment for the good of the kingdom of God. To disown, conceal, or sabotage our beauty does not glorify the God who entrusted us with such a treasure. Esther's beauty was not hidden; it was evident and opened a unique door of opportunity for her.

It seems that the king had banished his previous queen, Vashti, because she refused to appear when he called. Once his anger abated, he began the search for a new queen. Esther was among many beautiful women brought to his palace and quickly won the favor of the overseer.

After months of beauty treatments, Esther was presented to the king and won his affections. She was crowned the new queen and given a banquet. Can you imagine her radiantly shining? For added drama, the remainder of the second chapter of Esther describes how she actually saved the king's life by passing on information given to her by her uncle Mordecai regarding a plot to kill the king.

Esther was walking through each door that opened before her. We read of no hesitation, apology, or anxiety as her world became larger and her beauty more radiant, undoubtedly taking her far beyond anything she or her uncle had previously imagined.

We often underestimate what a challenge such a life and soul expansion can pose. Our older daughter, Jenna, lecturing at Curtain University in Perth, Australia, recently taught her largest class yet: 450 students. As she prepared the lecture, she spoke of being in an "existential crisis." She said, "I never defined myself as someone who could teach that many students at once."

Most of us can recall leaders, secular and within the church, at the pinnacle of success, making foolhardy personal choices that strip their lives of credibility and future opportunity. I suspect that perhaps some have failed to consciously engage a larger sense of self and so unconsciously have made self-sabotaging choices that whittled their lives to a more internally "manageable" size. To allow our identity to shift and change to accommodate, with integrity, a larger, more public or radiant role is no small task.

Sadly, the church has often been far too simplistic about the perils of such moments of shining, attributing these destructive, self-sabotaging choices completely to an inflated sense of self, to pride, or to the devil. Listening to my own life and those of hundreds of women, I have found a very different dynamic at work, one more rooted in self-contempt and self-sabotage than in self-inflation or an externalized evil force. It is not an easy or automatic choice to engage open doors that allow us to shine.

Unexpected External Challenges

For me, the unanticipated external challenge came in the form of Bobby's tumor; for Esther, it was an unexpected edict.

Her uncle Mordecai had made a powerful enemy when he refused to bow as Haman, one of the king's assistants, rode by. Haman was enraged and exacted revenge by prompting the king to sign an edict to kill not only Mordecai, but all Jews, young and old, women and children, on a soon-to-come appointed day.

Mordecai's response was to tear his clothes, don sackcloth and ashes, and wail loudly and bitterly. Soon we find him at the king's gate sending a plea for help to Esther. He asks her to go to the king, beg for mercy, and plead for her people. With our fairy-tale bubble completely burst, we learn from Esther that to approach the king without his initiating a summons could mean her death. Mordecai's reply seems to hold both personal threat and visionary imagination.

> When Hathach told Mordecai what Esther had said, Mordecai sent her this message: "Don't think that just because you live in the king's house you're the one Jew who will get out of this alive. If you persist in staying silent at a time like this, help and deliverance will arrive for the Jews from someplace else; but you and your family will be wiped out. Who knows? Maybe you were made queen for just such a time as this." (Esther 4:12–14 THE MESSAGE)

The Gift of a Unique Identity

In the previous few chapters, we have addressed how difficult it is to allow both our identity and creativity to actually be as uniquely individual as God has designed them to be. Anything that makes us stand out also makes us vulnerable to isolation. We fear that such individuality will lead to rejection, and being alone feels like death. Yet time and time again in Scripture we see how beautifully and specifically God uses our uniqueness for the good of the kingdom.

Think of Joseph. Though he was sold into slavery by his brothers, he landed (eventually) in the courts of Pharaoh, in a place where he could provide for his people in famine. Think of Moses. Who better to confront Pharaoh than a Jew with the full benefit of the finest education Egypt could offer? Think of Esther. As the Assyrian queen and a Jew, she was in a unique situation indeed. She had lived as an orphan in Mordecai's home. And her natural beauty set her apart. Perhaps both prepared her to live this unusual combination of identities with such grace.

Tragically, we often resist, hide, and even shame ourselves for being who we are. Think of the new mom back at work, who hesitates to talk too much about her baby, not sure whether she can be a professional and also a mom. Or the woman who spends most of her hours caring for children, but also landed her first big accounting contract and is not certain about mentioning it to other moms in her baby-sitting co-op. Or the female consultant who hesitates to talk with male colleagues about her intuition in a given situation, fearing she will be altogether dismissed.

Obviously, at times, wisdom calls for some discretion. Up until this moment, Mordecai has asked Esther not to announce her heritage and she has complied. Yet often it is fear, not wisdom, that motivates us to choose an alternating (being one person to one group and someone else to another) rather than integrated (being who we truly are at any given moment) identity. More often than not, when God calls us to shine, the opportunity invites us to be all of who we are, no matter how uncomfortable or politically incorrect that may be.

A Courageous Decision

Esther sent back her answer to Mordecai: "Go and get all the Jews living in Susa together. Fast for me. Don't eat or drink for three days, either day or night. I and my maids will fast with you. If you will do this, I'll go to the king, even though it's forbidden. If I die, I die."

Mordecai left and carried out Esther's instructions. (Esther 4:15–17 THE MESSAGE)

These verses represent a definite shift in our story. Until this moment, Mordecai was giving direction to Esther. Now we see that Esther has not only grown into a woman, but a courageous and decisive queen. Her role with Mordecai is reversed: Now she is giving the orders. Though she would go before the king alone, her instruction to fast shows her intention to go with the collective strength of her community's faith.

Wisely Using Emotional Intelligence

Esther not only needed courage, she also needed a wise and carefully considered approach.

Then the king asked, "What is it, Queen Esther? What is your request? Even up to half the kingdom, it will be given you."

"If it pleases the king," replied Esther, "let the king, together with Haman, come today to a banquet I have prepared for him."

"Bring Haman at once," the king said, "so that we may do what Esther asks."

So the king and Haman went to the banquet Esther had prepared. As they were drinking wine, the king again asked Esther, "Now what is your petition? It will be given you.

And what is your request? Even up to half the kingdom, it will be granted."

Esther replied, "My petition and my request is this: If the king regards me with favor and if it pleases the king to grant my petition and fulfill my request, let the king and Haman come tomorrow to the banquet I will prepare for them. Then I will answer the king's question." (Esther 5:3–8)

We might say that Esther was a very emotionally intelligent woman. She put her strength of relational knowledge to good use and recognized her feminine wisdom. We can only guess at the reality of her relationship with the king, but we do know that he had made at least two rash decisions before she was his queen: to banish the former queen and to sign Haman's edict. Esther knew how he operated and she worked that to her advantage. She fought emotional fire with emotional fire, creating not one but two banquets to cement a favorable climate for her pending request.

A Spirit of Power, Love, and Self-Discipline

Interestingly, the queen invited Haman to the banquet as well. Were the banquets designed to be her opportunity to meet him, to observe the dynamic between her enemy and the king? Had she mapped out the whole strategy or was she just getting all the players together? Perhaps she was applying common wisdom: "Keep your friends close and your enemies closer."

Esther's boldness echoes the wisdom the apostle Paul offered to young Timothy: "*For the Spirit God gave us does not make us timid, but gives us power, love and self-discipline*" (2 Timothy 1:7). In order to move away from fear, we move toward the traits that God has placed within us that are even more true and real than the circumstances that scare us. I hear all three in Esther's reply: power, love, and self-discipline.

It took courage to come face-to-face with Haman. As with her gutsy response to Mordecai, we see her embracing her power and taking advantage of her status as queen. We see a love for her people so great that she would risk her life. We see her self-control, her ability to be mindful of emotions, to artfully craft a plan in which emotions play a major role but not to be personally constrained by them.

Many of us are uncomfortable with the word *power*. As those gifted to effect change through gentler nurture and relationship, we tend toward softer, often more accurate descriptors like *influence*. Yet in times when we, like Esther, face life-and-death situations, awareness of the power of the Spirit of God within us can be critically important.

Leap and the Net Will Appear

While Esther was at work, so was God. Though her plan was well crafted, alone it was insufficient. During the night between Esther's two banquets (chapter 6), we read that the king could not sleep and ordered a scroll to be read. When the selected scroll told the story of his own life being saved by Esther's uncle, the king realized that Mordecai had not been rewarded. Immediately (and ironically), the king put Haman, Mordecai's archenemy, in charge of the task!

As far as we know, Esther had nothing to do with the king's bad night's sleep nor the selection of the text read to him that night. God was setting the stage in support of her coming appeal. One of the critical distinctions between shining and pride is the awareness of and reliance upon God. When we shine, we are not the end all, be all, do all. We are operating in tandem with God, yoked together, both headed in the same direction for the good of the kingdom. Remember that Esther called for fasting, an active choice that evidenced her dependence upon God. Even so, this was a moment where all she had done would clearly not be enough if God did not act. This moment required a leap of faith.

It was a moment of synchronicity, when the Spirit of God touched the situation and changed the dynamic forever. It was the moment Esther had been counting on. She knew God's intervention was both essential and beyond her control or ability to predict or guarantee. When we open ourselves to shining, we find ourselves in faith-stretching moments like these, both fully present and fully exposed, waiting in faith for God to act.

Unfortunately, many seek to use the essential ingredient of God's intervention to diminish the importance of our contribution. They translate our insufficiency into unimportance. Yet time and time again in Scripture, we see God calling his people to bring all of who they are—not nothingness and invisibility—into partnership with God for the larger good.

The Courage to Speak

There is a pattern of growth that we can observe in the stories of women in Scripture that moves them very consistently from invisibility to full presence and from silence to voice. Esther's story is no different.

So the king and Haman went to Queen Esther's banquet, and as they were drinking wine on the second day, the king again asked, "Queen Esther, what is your petition? It will be given you. What is your request? Even up to half the kingdom, it will be granted."

Then Queen Esther answered, "If I have found favor with you, Your Majesty, and if it pleases you, grant me my life—this is my petition. And spare my people—this is my request. For I and my people have been sold to be destroyed, killed and annihilated. If we had merely been sold as male and female slaves, I would have kept quiet, because no such distress would justify disturbing the king."

King Xerxes asked Queen Esther, "Who is he? Where is he—the man who has dared to do such a thing?"

Esther said, "An adversary and enemy! This vile Haman!"
(Esther 7:1–6)

Esther broke the rule of Southern feminine gentility: If you can't say something nice, don't say anything at all. She was ready not only with her very personally stated request, but also with an unapologetic and unwavering accusation against Haman. At this point, the king's rage took over; Haman was hanged. Later that same day, Esther again pleaded for her people and the king issued another edict that resulted in effective protection for the Jews.

Esther was transformed from a girl with the gift of beauty to a powerful queen effectively advocating for a nation. Hers was not an idyllic fairy tale, but one in which she encountered significant challenges both from without and within. We observe her spirit of power and love and self-control that overcame the self-sabotaging fear that undoubtedly threatened. We see her faith and a deep reliance upon God that enabled her to be all of who she was. If we will but listen to her story, we can begin to imagine a path of radiance for ourselves.

My Story (continued)

Within the course of a year, Bobby's tumor was radiated without incident and my book was edited with little compromise. That next fall found my husband, Bob, and I saying good-bye to our son, Bobby, as he returned to law school; our middle child, Jenna, as she left to complete her senior year of college; our youngest child, Betsy, as she entered college for the first time; and my beloved mother-in-law, Patsy, finally set free through death from the ravages of dementia. That same fall, Hurricane Rita visited our city. After being displaced for three weeks by evacuation orders, we came home to an intact house (Thanks be to God!) and a garage completely flattened by a fallen oak. Once again I was thankful that the book was not slated to be released until the following spring.

By the following March, I was very mindful of our calling to shine as well as how challenging it was to actually let that happen. When my friends wanted to throw a party for the book release, I let them. I even went to my favorite clothing store and paid full price for an outfit (I never pay full price!). The event was held at Amma's House, home of a nondenominational ministry to women. Sadly, the day of the event was also the day our community experienced the tragic death of two young women on our high school's soccer team. Many others were injured in the same bus accident, including Sarah, the daughter of my good friend Missy. After the party was over, I joined Missy at the hospital to wait with her and her husband as the first of Sarah's many surgeries was completed.

Once more I engaged both emotional poles in the same moment. This time, though, on the other side of our son's tumor journey, I realized that my soul could negotiate both extremes and not go crazy. It felt as if I was now grounded in my own experienced history, something akin to an emotional muscle memory. Somewhere along the way, I had redefined shining as something that was not idyllic theory or a fantasy of perfection, but instead moments large or small, happy and sad, rooted in deep awareness of my human experience of life and an equally profound sense of connection to God's divine presence.

Your *Story*

1. What is your emotional response to the idea of being called to shine? Excitement? Fear? Terror? Guilt?
2. What is your rational and theological response to the idea?
3. Review your answer to the question at the beginning of this chapter. Did you see that moment of shining as more idyllic or more human? Has your reflection about that moment been altered by these stories?
4. Can you think of a moment when you were radiant? Describe it in as much detail as you can, seeking to include all you recall about the context.
5. When you bring that memory to mind and speak about it, what do you feel?
6. Is there a part of your personal giftedness that you have dismissed or neglected? What would it look like to say yes to that gift within you? Name three specific actions.
7. Do you tend to alternate how you present yourself, stressing one part of who you are to one group and

another to another group? Is that a choice borne of wisdom or of fear? What would it look like to live in a more integrated way?

8. Who are you uniquely? Make a collage that includes important aspects of your identity, creativity, and radiance.

9. Spend some time in listening prayerful silence with God and your collage. Do you see/hear anything that surprises you? What is your emotional response to it? Is there a new wisdom or calling coming from the fullness of it? Celebrate the wonder of *you* alone with God and share your work with at least one other person.

CHOICES ALONG THE WAY

7

Choosing Vulnerability

*Fear is the cheapest room in the house,
I would like to see you living in better conditions.*[1]

HAFIZ

CONSIDER: When you feel unsafe around someone, what is the most common wall you raise? A steady stream of questions focused on others? Silence? Random chitchat? Busyness? A stiff manner or decorum? General avoidance? Aggression? Something else?

Carolyn

"Would you just get the #@&^ out of this &%^$#@ hospital room!?" Those words would have been shouted if Carolyn had had enough air in her lungs to make it happen. The harsh tone of her stern whisper was sufficient for me to discern that, even having just arrived and barely introduced myself, it was time for me to leave.

125

I had been kicked out of hospital rooms before, but it was never an experience I enjoyed. Working for several years in the capacity of a chaplain, I knew there was a story behind that response—a story I may or may not ever get to hear.

Carolyn had just been admitted to the medical intensive care unit in which I served as chaplain. Even before her nurse confirmed my suspicions, her brightly colored head scarf and very apparent shortness of breath told me that she was likely struggling with lung cancer. Only forty-six years old, Carolyn had definitely not planned on being anywhere close to the ICU that day.

I stood far enough outside of her room to be out of her line of vision and watched as nurses got her settled into the room and fulfilled the initial doctor's orders. She was sitting very straight in bed, leaning forward as lung patients often do. Muscles in her neck and chest were taut and straining for air even with the oxygen mask the nurse had placed around her ashen face. I noted on the chart that she was Catholic and had been seen by the priest in the emergency room. I said a silent prayer for this obviously suffering woman and went out to try to find her family in the waiting room.

It was easy to pick out her husband; his was the newest anxious face. As I located this middle-aged man flanked by two young women in their early twenties, I introduced myself and explained that the nurses were getting his wife settled. I assured them all that I would get them in to see her as soon as possible. His face relaxed a bit with the news. "I take it that this was an unexpected admission. Has Carolyn been in treatment for the cancer long?"

Many families waiting to see ICU patients were eager to talk. Offering the patient's history was one way they could be genuinely helpful, and sometimes it made the waiting pass more quickly. I learned that Carolyn had been fighting cancer for six months. The original diagnosis had been a shock. She was a nonsmoker, a healthy woman who cared well for both her family and herself. She was also a new grandmother of just three months.

Her husband went on to say that Carolyn had gotten a checkup nine months ago with a clean bill of health. It was the first time in many years that her doctor had not done a routine chest X ray, citing changes in insurance practices. "If only—" he said, with tears choking off his words.

"Those 'if only' thoughts really sting, don't they? They can be so hard to shake," I replied. I chatted for a few more minutes and then excused myself. "Let me go and see how they are coming with her admission." The nurses were ready for the family's visit, so I got them through the doors of the restricted unit, made initial introductions to the staff, and went on my way.

The next morning, I saved my visit to Carolyn's room until the end of my ICU rounds. She was alone, resting. Standing in her doorway, I waited until she looked up and then I asked if I could come in. She weakly nodded her affirmation. I was sad to see that her breathing was not much improved from the day before. She was, however, more relaxed—or perhaps simply fatigued. The dark lines under her eyes told me that the night had been difficult.

As I approached her bed, she reached out her hand and began to apologize for her behavior the day before. "*Shhh. Shhh,*" I responded, putting my index finger to my mouth. "Please, don't waste your precious breath and words on an unnecessary apology. You were understandably overwhelmed.

It was no time to meet another stranger. No offense taken. Really." Even as she smiled in relief, tears filled her eyes.

I took a seat next to her bed, waiting for her to catch her breath. Tears, even healing ones, come at quite a price for patients struggling for air. "I met your husband yesterday. And your daughters. They are so lovely and very concerned about you."

"Thanks," she said. "I really don't know what got into me yesterday." I couldn't tell if her tone was apologetic or self-reflective, or both.

"Really, there's no need to be concerned. None of us are ourselves when we are in crisis. You were suffering and scared, not to mention fighting to breathe! There's lots of compassion around here. It sounds like you would really like to understand what's going on inside of you. If that's the case, let's talk about it."

Carolyn responded, "The doctor caught me off guard yesterday morning. I'd gone in for my next dose of chemo. I had been more short of breath for several days, but was trying really hard to ignore it. I kept telling my husband it was a side effect of the chemo. But the nurse took one look at me and called the doctor, who examined me and told me he thought I had pneumonia, in addition to the cancer, or because of it. I had to come over here and be admitted to ICU right away. I was stunned and so angry." Feeling intense emotion, she closed her eyes and paused for a few moments.

Opening her eyes, she continued, "When you came in yesterday, I just couldn't stand the thought of another caring person coming to have pity on poor little me. I guess you're lucky in one way. If I had had the air, I would have really told you off." She almost laughed at her honest confession. The frank rapport and friendly, trusting banter between Carolyn and me was establishing quickly; ironically, it was likely because of her insulting remarks the day before.

"Okay, let me hear it. What did you *want* to say?"

"Really?" she asked.

"Really," I replied. "And don't think you are going to hurt my feelings or that it needs to make sense, either. I'd really like to know what you were thinking and feeling."

"Here goes." Carolyn caught her breath again as she closed her eyes. I could tell she was genuinely trying to go back to her experience of the day before, curiously, wisely, courageously. "What I wanted to say was, 'Who do you think you are? You don't know me. You don't care about me. You can't fix this. You're just as helpless as everyone else. Don't look at me that way and don't even *think* about coming in here. The last thing I need in my life is just one more person to disappoint and feel guilty about when I die.' " With that last sentence, Carolyn's eyes popped open, startled by her own words.

The Woman at the Well

In the course of life, having good boundaries is a necessary and healthy part of all relationships. Sometimes our boundaries are our friends, offering appropriate protection. But when we are wounded and frightened, sometimes we overuse them, sabotaging even healthy, life-giving relationships.

The story of the woman at the well can be seen as a story of a woman on the journey from self-sabotage to shining. Along the way, it seems that one hurdle she faced was that of the self-protective walls she had raised, intended to keep her heart safe but now shutting her off from the very One who could quench the deep thirst of her heart.

Taking the Initiative

When a Samaritan woman came to draw water, Jesus said to her, "Will you give me a drink?" (His disciples had gone into the town to buy food.) The Samaritan woman said to him, "You are a Jew and I am a Samaritan woman. How can you ask me for a drink?" (For Jews do not associate with Samaritans.) (John 4:7–9)

These opening verses of our story reveal Jesus taking the initiative, opening conversation with this woman. Such a move was surprising given the societal/religious tension between the Jews and the Samaritans. As always, though, Jesus lived to teach us that love is about relationship and connection, not compliance to isolating cultural mores.

This woman at the well wasn't shy. When Jesus made a simple request, she took some initiative of her own. Her reply seems pretty pointed—challenging at best, perhaps even contemptuous. Like many of us do when we are not feeling safe, she was seeking to nip this small kindness of initiated relationship in the bud. As if he didn't know the rules and she supported them, she said, *"You are a Jew and I am a Samaritan woman. How can you ask me for a drink?"*

I wish I could say that I've had no personal experience with this kind of quippy self-sabotage, but alas, it is one of my more common failures. As an introvert, I am often uncomfortable in social situations. In that discomfort, I have spoiled a potential relationship before it could begin more than once. It happened just the other day when a new acquaintance at church said, "Oh, you must be Bob's better half." To which I replied, without a sense of light banter, "Well, I'm not sure I'd say I'm better. He's a pretty good guy." To which the kind gentleman began to fumble, saying how much he liked my husband, and it was just a figure of speech. He has not spoken to me since, and frankly, I don't blame him. Like the woman at the well, even in simple conversation, my wall went up hard and fast.

The Wall of Contempt

Though Jesus persisted in kindness, this woman's next response can be seen as even more challenging and more openly contemptuous.

> *Jesus answered her, "If you knew the gift of God and who it is that asks you for a drink, you would have asked him and he would have given you living water."*
>
> *"Sir," the woman said, "you have nothing to draw with and the well is deep. Where can you get this living water? Are you greater than our father Jacob, who gave us the well and drank from it himself, as did also his sons and his livestock?" (John 4:10–12)*

It seems that the smaller she could make him, the safer she would feel. Though Jesus had initiated the conversation, this woman was clearly setting the tone. She let it be known right away that she was no fool. Her remarks were designed to put relational distance between herself and this strangely persistent man. Her verbal aggression placed her above him despite the social and religious realities of the day. Her words established her independence, competence, and arrogance. She maintained an identity that would keep him at a safe distance and her tender heart safely hidden from his sight, walled off from both potential damage and his healing touch.

Jesus Saw Thirst

Jesus answered, "Everyone who drinks this water will be thirsty again, but whoever drinks the water I give them will never thirst. Indeed, the water I give them will become in them a spring of water welling up to eternal life."

The woman said to him, "Sir, give me this water so that I won't get thirsty and have to keep coming here to draw water." (John 4:13–15)

But the only thing this rabbi wanted to talk about was thirst . . . and water, a never-ending supply of water. The woman at the well couldn't even imagine the possibility.

It appears that Jesus saw through the hard outer shell of arrogant competence. Perhaps he concluded that if she was coming to draw water now, in the heat of the day, it was likely she was avoiding the company of the women often gathered here when it was cooler. Her independence was perhaps more survival instinct or necessity than preference. It must have left her thirsty at a far deeper level than she knew. Her sabotaging contempt did not seem to work with him. He saw the tender woman beneath the harsh words.

Jesus had the wisdom and benefit of being a healthy, well-differentiated person. He knew that all he had offered, and would continue to offer, was kindness. He knew that her responses were more about her than about him. Rather than taking on this criticism, he listened to the message it offered him about the woman who spoke it, a message much deeper than could be discerned on the surface. He did not react to her contempt; he responded to her hurting heart. He saw thirst and steadfastly offered relief.

I would guess that the way Jesus held her gaze said even more than his words. It must have been hopelessly uncomfortable, disturbing, unsettling . . . and oddly drawing; she did not choose to leave. Notice her imperative, commanding words: *"Sir, give me this water . . ."*

Jesus Invited Her to Be Authentically Known

He told her, "Go, call your husband and come back."
"I have no husband," she replied.
Jesus said to her, "You are right when you say you have no husband. The fact is, you have had five husbands, and the man you now have is not your husband. What you have just said is quite true." (John 4:16–18)

It's a dance most of us do to some extent: wanting to be known and hiding for fear of being known, choosing vulnerability and backing away from it. This woman at the well appears to know it well. When Jesus told her to call her husband, she replied with something that was technically true but far from the whole story. A dance of hide-and-seek. The parts she was hiding were parts of her story that held pain and quite possibly shame for her.

Again, it is important to be cautious about attaching a moral conclusion to her response. We have no idea what her circumstances might be. As we've mentioned before, women in that culture had precious little social power of any sort; with that reality, we need to be hesitant to hold her responsible for her history with men. Also, the five previous relationships were *husbands*.

It seems to me, however, the technical morality of this moment is much less the issue than this woman's *perception* of it. The combination of her walls, her shaming contempt toward Jesus, and her half-truth here seems to say that, guilty or not, she was *feeling* overwhelming shame. Shame is often the reason we hide and wall ourselves off from others. It isolates us and makes us believe that we are the only "defective" ones. It seeks to convince us that we are hopelessly flawed, perhaps even a danger and genuine threat to those who might successfully scale our walls.

Counterintuitively, shame often has little to do with actual moral guilt. A common evidence of this is in cases of child abuse. Despite their obvious innocence, persistent shame is often the most difficult and tenacious wound that victims of abuse battle. Many of us also experience this dynamic on a daily basis. We may feel shame for not having the body of a twenty-year-old when we are fifty. Or we might feel shame for poor choices our adult children make quite apart from us. We can feel shame for feeling fatigued at the end of a sixty-hour workweek or for taking a well-deserved vacation. Our shame does not have to be justified or rational to be real and destructive. Wisely, Jesus knew the best antidote for shame is authentic relationship.

Speaking Shame

Jesus took the truth within the response this woman gave him, affirmed it, and spoke the parts of her story she was avoiding. He said it, the whole of it, and didn't flinch. Or run. Or likely even change the way he looked at her. The contempt, judgment, and distance she expected, the isolation and abandonment that she may have felt from everyone she'd ever known, especially herself, did not happen here. The self-sabotaging shame she had been hiding behind evaporated. Her destructive identity that kept others at bay, protecting and isolating her heart, melted away.

Might she have been thinking, *Never mind how he knew . . . who cares? He knew and didn't leave . . . didn't even shift his eyes.* Jesus saw her, with the whole truth and painful reality of her story, and nothing changed. This man was different.

As with the story of the woman caught in adultery, Jesus never addressed or challenged or corrected the issue sometimes assumed to be sexual impropriety. He only challenged the walls, the secrets, and the shame at the root of the self-destructive, isolating behavioral choices. As noted previously, these relationship-sabotaging, internally destructive dynamics are often very similar in a woman who is a victim of abuse or in an adult who chooses sexual misconduct.

The Emptiness of Religion

"Sir," the woman said, "I can see that you are a prophet. Our ancestors worshiped on this mountain, but you Jews claim that the place where we must worship is in Jerusalem."

"Woman," Jesus replied, "believe me, a time is coming when you will worship the Father neither on this mountain nor in Jerusalem. You Samaritans worship what you do not know; we worship what we do know, for salvation is from the Jews. Yet a time is coming and has now come when the true worshipers will worship the Father in the Spirit and in truth, for they are the kind of worshipers the Father seeks. God is spirit, and his worshipers must worship in the Spirit and in truth." (John 4:19–24)

Yes, indeed, this strange rabbi was different; uncomfortably different. He must be a prophet. There she goes again . . . the dance continues. It appears that when Jesus comes close to her heart, she knows it, feels it, and hits reverse as quickly as she can. Think sabotage.

In chapter 3 of this book, we saw Martha initiating what looked like a very similar conversation with Jesus: one focused on right thinking and right belief. Such dialogue sought to move each of these women away from vulnerable, beating, bleeding human hearts into the safe place of concepts and ideas. As we described, while such conversation can be helpful and important, in the context of the dynamics of this story, it looks like an empty diversion. As he had done with Martha, Jesus let the woman lead. Also like Martha, the woman tried to make sure the conversation stayed in the aloof place of the unknowable future.

The woman said, "I know that Messiah" (called Christ) "is coming. When he comes, he will explain everything to us." (John 4:25)

The Healing Nature of Connection

Then Jesus declared, "I, the one speaking to you—I am he." (John 4:26)

How long did they stand there? I wonder if her posture straightened. She was suddenly no longer the shameful one to be avoided; she was the *only* one in town to whom the Messiah had spoken. I wonder how long it took her to connect the dots: *He did know more about me than he should have. Maybe he is the Messiah. Wait . . . the Messiah talked to me? Asked me for water? Oh no! I guess I was a little sassy, wasn't I . . . but it didn't matter. Clearly, it didn't matter. He knows a lot worse about me than that. He knows it all. And still, he stayed to speak to me? And even told me who he was? And those eyes . . . what do I do with those eyes?*

Shame isolates. When we elect isolation, we are almost always sabotaging our own healing. Authentic connection heals. This is the fruit of a wise choice for vulnerability. It is important to choose *wisely* those with whom we share our shame. As we noted in the opening, boundaries are not all bad; they can rightly protect our hearts at times. Choosing authenticity carelessly or unwisely can actually be another form of self-sabotage, an attempt to prove to ourselves, once again, that the world is unsafe.

A Revealing Celebration

Then, leaving her water jar, the woman went back to the town and said to the people, "Come, see a man who told me everything I ever did. Could this be the Messiah?" . . .

Many of the Samaritans from that town believed in him because of the woman's testimony, "He told me everything I ever did." (John 4:28–29, 39)

I just love the details of her response. First, she left her water jar. It seems that life as she knew it had ended; water was no longer a priority. Her thirst had been met at a far deeper level. Both her old sense of herself and the routine that accompanied it were done.

Notice the depth of the change: She *went looking* for the people she had likely been avoiding by her noontime visit to the well. When she found them, she actually celebrated that Jesus knew everything she'd ever done. Clearly, the towns-people knew the details of her living situation—details she avoided telling Jesus. Suddenly those particulars became the substance of her testimony? She was celebrating that this man knew her *whole* story, even *those* things about her? And she was inviting them to meet this one who knew all and was unafraid to tell all?

The woman who was alone and full of contempt had become one who was celebrating being fully known. What a transformation! She was standing in all of her authenticity and humanity, beloved and free. Shining for all to see, her glow was an effective testimony that transformed her community: Many believed.

Carolyn (continued)

"That's it," Carolyn said. "I feel guilty, ashamed really, that I may be dying. That just seems weird. Am I crazy?"

"Oh no, you're not crazy at all," I offered as reassuringly as I could. "As strange as it seems, it's a pretty common way for us to deal with really, really sad things."

"I am so tired of being sad . . . and angry," Carolyn continued with a short-breathed sigh. "I've been so angry with everyone. My family would not at all have been surprised by the way I treated you. Really, I don't know what's gotten into me."

"Some cancer patients find themselves trying to distance themselves from people, putting up walls of all kinds between themselves and the people they love," I explained, trying to speak slowly enough for her to follow a very complicated human dynamic. "Feeling ashamed . . . and even behaving badly to support that feeling is one way. It's really an attempt to make the possibility of having to say good-bye seem easier."

"Like self-sabotage, you mean? Or what my mom used to call 'cutting your nose off to spite your face'?" Carolyn grinned.

"You sound pretty well informed about all these games we play," I noted.

"I used to have a counseling practice . . . in another life," Carolyn explained. "I guess it's harder for me to see my own stuff."

"I think maybe you've been a little preoccupied, say, with breathing?" I added.

The next time I saw Carolyn, she was in a much different place physically, emotionally, and spiritually.

"The good news is that the pneumonia has cleared much faster than they thought it would," Carolyn said. "The bad news is that they can't say yet whether the chemo is working," she stated matter-of-factly. "Listen, I wanted to thank you for our conversation the other day. It helped. I just decided then and there, that very day actually, that nothing was going to steal even one more minute from my family and me. Now, I haven't given up, I am hoping for many, many more years, Lord willing. But even if that's not the way it's going to be, I am not donating one more minute to self-sabotage. No walls. If being my vulnerable and real and open and connected self is too sad, we'll just be 'too sad' together. I intend to stay as fully connected as I can for as long as I can." Though tears brimmed, Carolyn's voice was beautifully firm and clear. "I'm back to being my old self, my real self. Thank you."

"Hey, wait a minute, you did all the hard work," I said with a smile.

"You are so right. I'll thank myself, too." Carolyn winked and laughed.

Your *Story* ———————————

1. Think back to your answer to our opening question. Write/tell one story of how you used a wall appropriately. Write/tell another about when you think you hid behind a wall to your own detriment.

2. What kind of situations scare you the most? Intimacy? Shared grief? Anger (yours or another's)? Joy? Compliments?

3. Talk about a time when you behaved poorly but someone saw through your wall to the pain beneath. What were you feeling? How did you respond?

4. What are you thirsting for? Where are you looking for water? How is your current approach working?

5. Prayerfully consider: What are your secrets? Are any of them making you sick?

6. When have you felt most alone in your life? To what degree were shame and self-erected walls involved in your isolation?

7. Seek to become aware of moments when you feel shame in the coming week. Look for physical evidence, such as covering your face, a flushed face, a churning stomach, a cold sweat. You might find yourself using less direct descriptors, such as *embarrassed, humiliated,* or *I just wanted to die.* Talk through one moment with a safe person.

8. Imagine yourself standing with Jesus at Jacob's well. Sketch the scene to more completely enter it. He says to you, "I, the one speaking to you—I am he." What do you see on his face? Hear in his voice? Describe your response: feelings, thoughts, words, actions. Do any secrets or feelings of shame surface for you?

8

Choosing to Say No

Women's Confession

*We have followed too little
the devices and desires
of our own hearts.*

*We have abandoned ourselves
to the disservice of others.*

*We have not included ourselves
in the quest for justice and joy.*

*We hold ourselves responsible
for saying the debilitating Yes
again and again without restraint.*

*We hold ourselves responsible
for not saying the life-giving No
time after time.*

May all this and more be amended.
Amen.[1]

ALLA RENÉE BOZARTH

CONSIDER: When was the last time you told someone (other than a child) *no*, knowing full well that they would be at least disappointed and possibly even punish you for your decision? Write or tell the story.

Tonya

"It's just not working anymore," Tonya said, eyes cast down and forehead wrinkled in confusion. Those were the first words she spoke after I opened our time together with a prayer, a lighted candle, and a few minutes of silence. It seemed like she was talking more to herself than to me: "Why in the world is it not working anymore?"

"Can you be more specific?" I asked after a moment. "What isn't working?"

As if startled from a daze, she said, "I'm sorry. Of course. You have no idea what I'm talking about, do you! It's just that when I stopped for a minute to actually put words to why I'm here, I think I understood why I made this appointment for the first time myself."

Tonya and I were beginning spiritual direction. Dressed in a crisp, open-collared blouse, she appeared self-assured, a very put-together woman in her mid-forties. She sat straight in her chair with clear, quick, bright eyes. She told me in our previous introductory meeting that she was seeking spiritual direction in preparation for a sabbatical she had scheduled for the following school year, a full year from our first

142

appointment. As a tenured and very popular local university professor with twenty years of teaching under her belt, she had twice before declined the university's offer of such time and space. This time things were different. Here's my recollection of the remainder of our conversation.

"It's just not working anymore . . . none of it is. My marriage, my teaching, my spiritual life, my friendships . . . none of it is working. That sounds rash, doesn't it? Overstated?" she questioned, unsure of her perspective.

"It's only overstated if it's not the reality," I offered. "From my experience, many women tend to *understate* rather than overstate when life is not working."

"Really," she replied slowly, as if absorbing an unexpected truth. I could tell by the pace of our conversation that Tonya was fully engaged. It seemed that she was turning her well-honed researching skills inward. I waited until she was ready to continue.

"I don't know where to start," she said.

"One thing I've learned after doing this for a while is that it doesn't much matter where you start, we will likely end up talking about what's most important," I replied. "How about this: From the list you offered, what seems to be working the least well *today*?"

"That's easy: my marriage. This morning my husband and I had a huge fight over my initial plans for my sabbatical. I want to spend the first six months in England doing research and then take a month to travel before I come home. I plan to do a walking tour of some monasteries. You would think I was planning to go to the moon the way he reacted!" She was no longer reflective but leaning forward in her chair with a lot of energy.

Tonya continued, "You don't know me, but I am not a violent person. I actually threw my shoe at him when he said to me, 'Who do you think you are? A twenty-something hippie chick backpacking through Europe? You don't want to go gallivanting around on your own!' Who is he to say what I want and don't want? Just because we've always done vacations together doesn't mean we always have to, right?"

She paused to take a breath, perhaps a little surprised at her own intensity. "Really, this isn't about him. I love being married to Tim. We've never had kids; it's just the two of us, and we have a great time together. I'm not doing this because I'm mad or anything like that . . . well, at least I wasn't mad, until now." Her shoulders slumped like a deflated balloon and she became quiet.

"Where do you think he might have gotten the idea that you wouldn't enjoy the lone adventure?" I queried.

"I'm sure it's from me. And he's right. Up until now, I wouldn't have. I've hated to travel alone for as long as I can remember. But I want to now. In fact, I think this situation with him is a good example of why so many things are not working in my life right now," Tonya said, connecting the dots as she spoke.

"For instance, my dean was surprised that I was planning to actually take the sabbatical next year. When my first one came around, I refused it. Can you believe that? Refusing a year off with pay? I had hit such a good rhythm with my teaching. I had won the university's excellence in teaching award the previous year. When the next sabbatical offer came, I was in the middle of a critical moment with my research. I also loved the grad students I had at the time. Both times, it felt as if I was riding this perfect wave and I was afraid to mess it up. Anyway, he was really surprised last week at the faculty meeting when I said I was taking this one."

"Say more about how that connects with your marriage," I pressed. "I'm not quite sure I understand."

"It's just that I used to do it one way. I always travel with people and refuse sabbaticals. Now things have changed, but no one but me sees it. And when I say it, they don't hear me or they act shocked or weird or something. Here's another example of the same thing. I need a new small group at church. For years, I've been in a group where I have by and large been the one leading—not officially, it just happened. But I've realized that I don't really want to be in charge anymore. I don't know what changed—it just did. Again, I drop hints here and there and no one picks up on it." The more Tonya saw a theme forming, the more frustrated she became.

"So, your sweet Southern polite hints and suggestions aren't doing the trick?" I clarified.

"No, they're not, not at all. Not with anybody. But I really hate to be horsey about it all," she added with a wince.

"Can you say what you mean by *horsey*?" I asked.

"It's an expression my mom always used. Kind of like pushy, aggressive, rude, bully-like," Tonya explained.

"Would you say that in your own personal, internal definitions, to directly tell someone no is inconsiderate and rude, horsey?" I suggested.

"I don't really want to admit it, but I think I do feel that way. So you're saying that maybe the reason I feel like my life is not working is because all these people in all these different areas of my life aren't hearing me when I try to tell them about how I've changed or how what I want or need has changed? And the reason they aren't hearing me is because I sabotage myself by how I communicate? Maybe I'm just not willing, or maybe I don't even know *how* to just tell them no?" she proffered.

"Only you can answer that one. Does that describe what's happening?" I asked.

"Yes, I think it does. Even though I'm able to recognize how things shift for me and how what I want is changing, I have a hard time asking other people to really take the change seriously. It's like I need to say a clear no to the old way of being before I can really be different. And if I waffle with that no, I sabotage my own growth. Maybe I have a hard time really taking these changes seriously myself—or even taking myself seriously. Ugh, let's not go there," Tonya said with a sly smile, clearly relieved that she was beginning to see some patterns to what had begun as a tangled ball of assorted and seemingly random frustrations.

Hannah

Hannah's story begins as one of many stories of infertility in Scripture. Trapped in suffering and loss of hope, we first observe her passivity and silence.

Saying No to the Old Patterns of Home

There was a certain man . . . whose name was Elkanah. . . . He had two wives; one was called Hannah and the other Peninnah. Peninnah had children, but Hannah had none.

Year after year this man went up from his town to worship and sacrifice to the Lord Almighty at Shiloh, where Hophni and Phinehas, the two sons of Eli, were priests of the Lord. Whenever the day came for Elkanah to sacrifice, he would

give portions of the meat to his wife Peninnah and to all her
sons and daughters. But to Hannah he gave a double portion
because he loved her, and the Lord had closed her womb.
Because the Lord had closed Hannah's womb, her rival kept
provoking her in order to irritate her. This went on year after
year. Whenever Hannah went up to the house of the Lord,
her rival provoked her till she wept and would not eat. Her
husband Elkanah would say to her, "Hannah, why are you
weeping? Why don't you eat? Why are you downhearted?
Don't I mean more to you than ten sons?"

Once when they had finished eating and drinking in Shiloh,
Hannah stood up. (1 Samuel 1:1–9)

Except for the last three words, we find Hannah coping
with the pain of her infertility through compliance and passivity. Though provoked by Peninnah, she did not speak or
move or defend herself in any way; she only wept and refused
to eat. When questioned by Elkanah, she began to eat and
drink with the others. It does not appear as an independent
choice but rather compliance, the choice of no choice.

"Hannah stood up." This is the first of two hinge points
of change in our story. A nonverbal body language clue: she
stood. With that simple action, Hannah's whole world shifted.
She began to act independently. She was born as a creative
individual, a person of will and intention. She left the ruts of
passivity and paralytic, unthinking compliance. She began
to say no to her old way of doing life.

Interestingly, for a different woman, with another way of
securing herself in life, such a beginning change point might
have looked very different. Think of Martha in her story from
chapter 3 of this book. Unthinking compliance for her was
not passivity but service, service, and more service. Mary was

the one in that story who made the noncompliant choice to sit. The issue is not the specifics of the pattern; the issue is choosing life over death, finding strength within ourselves to live our own lives.

Because we are living beings, God is continually moving us toward new growth. In that process, we are often called to question our unthinking or autopilot modes of being, our default patterns, our ruts, and our habits, whatever those might be. Without such active inquiry, patterns that once brought life may now keep us from it. We trade a vital, God-inspired life for a wooden idol of mere existence. Our made-in-the-image-of-God personhood is day by day, bit by bit, surrendered to a dull and infertile existence, a far cry from the abundant life to which we are called.

Saying No to Old Patterns With God

Once when they had finished eating and drinking in Shiloh, Hannah stood up. Now Eli the priest was sitting on his chair by the doorpost of the Lord's house. In her deep anguish Hannah prayed to the Lord, weeping bitterly. And she made a vow, saying, "Lord Almighty, if you will only look on your servant's misery and remember me, and not forget your servant but give her a son, then I will give him to the Lord for all the days of his life, and no razor will ever be used on his head." (1 Samuel 1:9–11)

When Hannah stood in defiance of her former passivity, she intuitively moved toward God. The descriptors the writer uses of her are very intense, providing us with a sense of contrast to the passive "before" image: bitterness of soul, *much* weeping, and praying with a vow. There is movement and stirring, externally and internally.

We know from previous verses that Hannah went to the temple yearly and was supplied with an offering by Elkanah; but we have no sense of where she herself was in relationship with God. I wonder if she prayed. Pleaded? Bargained? Vowed? Had she quit praying as passivity and deadness, hopelessness and discouragement invaded her heart?

When you think about it, it takes a bit of moxie to bargain with *the Lord Almighty*. Yet that's what Hannah did as she began to pray. She was not just standing and moving to the temple, she was standing, figuratively speaking, toe-to-toe, face-to-face, seeking to strike a bargain with God. Though many of us want to duck for cover at such a bold move, the reality is that this moment of strong personhood and engagement on Hannah's part is common to many stories of growing and godly women in Scripture.

One of the most surprising dynamics in my own spiritual life is that the longer I walk in relationship with God, the more God seems to invite me to be present in a larger and larger way within the relationship. I was taught to think it might have worked the other way. That is, that the more I knew of God, the smaller I would feel and the more I would surrender to the point of nothingness. In Hannah's story, the direction of growth is definitely away from passivity, compliance, and invisibility and toward personhood, desire, and voice. The kind of relational shift now evident in her stance before God is about to show up in even more ways.

Saying No to Untrue Labels

As she kept on praying to the Lord, Eli observed her mouth. Hannah was praying in her heart, and her lips were moving but her voice was not heard. Eli thought she was drunk and said to her, "How long are you going to stay drunk? Put away your wine."

"Not so, my lord," Hannah replied, "I am a woman who is deeply troubled. I have not been drinking wine or beer; I was pouring out my soul to the Lord. Do not take your servant for a wicked woman; I have been praying here out of my great anguish and grief." (1 Samuel 1:12–16)

Eli made a false assumption: *"Eli thought she was drunk."* He not only made the assumption, he also projected this moment beyond the present and assumed it was a habit: *"How long are you going to stay drunk?"* As if that were not enough, he dared to provide her with a solution: *"Put away your wine."*

It appears God made sure Hannah had ample justification to speak up for herself. She had taken on God in her prayer, so Eli was easy. Likely for the first time in her life, she refused false presumptions about her identity and fought for the right to define herself.

With a new and amazing sense of inner authority, she named both who she was and who she was not; what she had been doing and what she had not been doing. It is an odd paradox that in this moment of unapologetically acknowledging her undiminished pain, grief, and anguish, she was stronger than ever before. Her pain and emotion did not produce the weakness or fragility that we as women often fear; Hannah's desperately raw authenticity birthed a grounded presence and powerfully clear voice.

Saying No to the Voice of Authority

Eli answered, "Go in peace, and may the God of Israel grant you what you have asked of him."

> She said, "*May your servant find favor in your eyes.*" *Then she went her way and ate something, and her face was no longer downcast.* (1 Samuel 1:17–18)

I love the immense healing power of these stories of women in Scripture. Did you see what happened in verse 15 in the section prior to this one? The first *spoken* words (though we do have her unspoken prayer) this saintly woman uttered were to say no to a *man,* to a *priest,* a voice of *authority* in her world! Though I do not think the significance of that escaped the writer or Jewish reader, I believe that there are radical and healing messages in stories like this that modern readers often miss.

It is important to note both Hannah's willingness to say no to Eli and her desire for his favor. So often we are taught that to openly disagree with a person in authority, even to correct them, is the same as disrespecting or refusing their authority. Though Hannah clearly disagreed with Eli and let him know it, she also clearly respected him and not only honored his authority but sought and received his blessing!

This story also holds an important image for women who seek to grow. Many of us have been given and actively received authoritative and false messages based on untrue assumptions. A critical and, from my observation, generally unavoidable point in our growth comes as we begin to find, accept, and speak the kind of inner authority and God-and-me-alone self-definition that Hannah discovers here.

Saying No to Collective Direction, Starvation, and Shame

Then she went her way and ate something, and her face was no longer downcast. (1 Samuel 1:18)

151

This is the second of the two critical hinge points of Hannah's story. In the first, *Hannah stood up*; Hannah acknowledged and lived her individual identity, her personhood, first with God and then with Eli. In this second hinge point, *she went her way*; Hannah began to live that individual identity and force of will forward into her daily existence.

Step one of that journey was eating. I love it! The first thing Hannah noticed was that she was hungry and so she ate. How different this organic hunger response feels compared to her eating as compliance earlier. Learning the importance of self-care is one of the first challenges for women who begin to grow.

Step two was that her face was no longer downcast. A downcast face is a universal image for shame. Though the world is more open to women than ever before, including most of those who read this book, many continue to hear messages from near and far, and often from within, that say that to be a woman is to be less than a man. In subtle ways, some still live with their faces downcast. God wants us all to be just like Hannah, to walk forward into the world with a face that is no longer downcast, standing tall, looking up and around, radiant for all to see.

Saying No to Her Husband

Early the next morning they arose and worshiped before the Lord and then went back to their home at Ramah. Elkanah made love to his wife Hannah, and the Lord remembered her. So in the course of time Hannah became pregnant and gave birth to a son. She named him Samuel, saying, "Because I asked the Lord for him."

When her husband Elkanah went up with all his family to offer the annual sacrifice to the Lord and to fulfill his vow,

Hannah did not go. She said to her husband, "After the boy is weaned, I will take him and present him before the Lord, and he will live there always."

"Do what seems best to you," her husband Elkanah told her. "Stay here until you have weaned him; only may the Lord make good his word." So the woman stayed at home and nursed her son until she had weaned him. (1 Samuel 1:19–23)

Interestingly, the writer almost downplays the actual answer to Hannah's prayer: "*So in the course of time.*" Also notable, perhaps even scandalous: Hannah named the son. Naming was done almost exclusively by men. Not only did she name him, she claimed that he was an answer to *her* prayer. As if that were not enough to establish Hannah's now independently experienced relationship with God, the writer continues with Hannah's refusal to go to the annual sacrifice.

She'd always gone before. It had been a place of both torture and eventual triumph for her. That was then; this was now. She had a plan and she was sticking to it. She spoke with clarity and definitively. Her husband consented. To be truthful, I have no idea what to make of his response ("*only may the Lord make good his word*").

When I lead women's retreats, I often have an opportunity to tell the story of our family's decision to move from Texas to Seattle for my graduate education. Women sometimes approach me saying, "Oh, my husband would never agree to that. You are so lucky." Though I do not in any way diminish the rare and significant sacrifices my husband and children made, that response by women is often based on convenient assumptions more than fact. In essence, they are saying that their scope of possibilities in the kingdom and even obedience to God is significantly limited by their controlling, uncooperative husbands—and that is a reality they support.

We often *assume* that our families would be uncooperative as a way of shortcutting the sometimes painful and frightening possibility that God might indeed be calling us to a daring life adventure. As gifted nurturers, we struggle to dare to *have* a separate sense of calling. If we get that far, to seriously ask someone to sacrifice for our sense of calling is often beyond what we will dare to *hear* from God, much less speak aloud or act upon. And if we get to the point of asking, we may approach them with nonnegotiable, unrealistic demands or, at the opposite extreme, a let-me-make-it-easy-for-you-to-say-no attitude. They simply fulfill the response we have set them up to offer. I know these dynamics well because I've used them all. Think self-sabotage.

To be clear, many women who have said no to their husbands have suffered great material, physical, or relational loss, even punishment. But it seems unfair, ungrounded, and self-sabotaging to assume the same would be so for the vast majority of married women.

Saying No to Social Norms

After he was weaned, she took the boy with her, young as he was, along with a three-year-old bull, an ephah of flour and a skin of wine, and brought him to the house of the Lord at Shiloh. When the bull had been sacrificed, they brought the boy to Eli, and she said to him, "Pardon me, my lord. As surely as you live, I am the woman who stood here beside you praying to the Lord. I prayed for this child, and the Lord has granted me what I asked of him. So now I give him to the Lord. For his whole life he will be given over to the Lord." And he worshiped the Lord there. (1 Samuel 1:24–28)

Note the number of times *I* is used. Once more, Hannah's independent relationship with God is emphasized. Remember that as our story began, Elkanah gave Hannah the sacrifices she was to offer; now she brought her own. We cannot truly give that which we do not truly possess. The same is true regarding Hannah's son; as the answer to her prayer, she saw him as hers to give. I can think of nothing more challenging to offer than a child so young. Yet the faith of this woman, now rooted in her personal experience of God rather than authorities or surrogates, was strong enough to bear the weight of that challenge with vision and song (1 Samuel 2:1–10).

Tonya (continued)

Over her pre-sabbatical year, Tonya and I covered a lot of ground. We celebrated how aware she was of her own internal shifts, the good and very active work of God's Spirit within. We acknowledged how surprisingly ambivalent we sometimes feel about good and welcome change, chiefly because it also unavoidably brings loss into our lives. Wisdom asks us to actively let go of old ways of living in order to become the women God has created us to be. Saying no is often the first step toward saying yes to new life.

In our work together, Tonya used her astute reflective capabilities to assemble a detailed description of who she was before and how she had changed. In naming more concretely what was the same and what was different, she became clearer about those aspects of her former life she wanted to release.

As we explored the grief inherent to growth, we also noted how such sadness and ambivalence can cause us to communicate double messages to the people around us, resulting in messes of all sorts. From time to time, Tonya and I would actually rehearse and experiment with how it felt to directly say no, or other times, an enthusiastic *yes!* Tonya learned that her speech could be not only direct but kind, considerate of herself and of others. The more she worked, the more her words matched her life. As she expressed herself directly, sometimes the powerful sense of her own personhood scared her.

Tonya also grew in awareness of her previous doublespeak. In more direct communication, she and her husband worked through his concerns about her trip relatively quickly. He also acknowledged some of his unspoken, more self-centered, concerns. By the time she was ready to leave, Tonya began her journey abroad with a full, free, and very expectant heart.

Your *Story*

1. Review your answer to our opening question. Thinking back, how did you feel in that moment? Do you see it any differently in light of Tonya or Hannah's stories?
2. Have you, like Hannah, ever become passive in the midst of suffering? Did that passivity spread to other areas of your life?
3. Can you recall a time when you were seeking to change and those around you did not hear you or resisted your efforts? Do you notice any ambivalence within yourself that might have been sending them mixed messages?

4. Think of a time when you spoke *no* very directly. How did you feel? What would your mother/grandmother have said about the moment?

5. Have you ever had another person make a false assumption about you? How did you react internally? Externally? Have you ever been misunderstood? How did you respond?

6. Can you think of times in your life that echo the major life shifts reflected in Hannah's story? *Hannah stood up* and *she went her way*. Describe one of these times.

7. What kinds of people, circumstances, or situations are the most challenging for you to say no to?

8. Read Hannah's song (1 Samuel 2:1–10). What stands out to you in it? How would you describe the identity of the woman who would write such a poem? In what ways do you connect with her?

9

Choosing to Tell Your Story

The biggest thing I had to overcome was this voice inside that said, "If you do this you'll kill yourself, you'll get killed." It was just so loud. And stepping across that inner voice was really traumatic for me. I discovered that if you don't cross that line, you never meet yourself; you never become who you can be unless you can get past your socialization, where that older generation has told you what they had learned about survival. You actually have to break ranks with it, or you will never meet yourself. And it's like stepping outside of a safety zone, and it is very hard to do. But if you ever do it, you always know how to risk your life.[1]

BERNICE JOHNSON REAGON

CONSIDER: When did you last tell your story to another? How did you feel after you told it? Was it something you enjoyed? Dreaded? Experienced with indifference? Felt shame about? Experienced with gratitude?

Growing up in a suburban neighborhood in the early sixties, I have many memories of my mother and neighborhood women gathered at our small kitchen table, smoking
cigarettes and drinking coffee. Though I have no memory of
the actual conversations, the tones were friendly and caring.
I never knew the power of such routine connection until I
joined a circle of women who met regularly to tell our stories and to listen to one another. Here is one story that I
heard from a woman we will call Lori. The prompt we were
responding to that evening was to speak about a time when
we found unexpected healing in telling our story.

Lori

"I am a copy editor, and all day long my job is to improve
the things that other people write. Being an English major
and detail person, I'm pretty good at what I do. But a few
months ago I noticed that I have been too willing to allow
my job to overshadow my own writing. And I really do feel
called to write. So I made a deal with God last month that
the next call for submissions I ran across would be my first
assignment. No excuses. No more self-sabotage.

"Well, last week, I was reading this small but really well
done quarterly publication from a local Christian women's
center. I've read it for years, but had never noticed a call for
submissions until this issue. I guess I ignored what I wasn't
ready to see. Anyway—oh, and this is important—I had
picked it up while I was eating lunch in the middle of my
absolutely disastrous bedroom. I was painting, so I moved
all the furniture to the center and covered it with old sheets.
I managed to get the first coat on before lunch but wanted

to eat in the room . . . I know I'm crazy . . . just to enjoy the new color.

"So there I was: loving the new green on the walls, in the middle of this mess, eating lunch and reading. There it was: the call for submissions I had been waiting for. But when I started to read about the topic, I nearly backed out. Can you believe it? They wanted mother/daughter stories."

At this point, there was a collective groan in the room. We all knew Lori had a very painful relationship with her mother.

"I threw down my sandwich and the magazine and bolted out the door. I was way too angry to sit. I felt totally tricked by God. And believe me, I objected loud and clear.

"I knew they didn't want a story like mine. No one wants to hear a story full of shame and pain; everyone wants a happy ending. I don't have this idyllic story of wonderful nurturing and connection. I was sure that was what they were looking for . . . upbeat, inspiring stuff. Not pain, especially not unresolved, real-time pain. Why spend the time writing something no one wants to read? I was sure it wouldn't be accepted! Why set myself up for rejection? Wouldn't *that* be self-sabotage?"

Lori stopped and took a deep breath. Tears filled her eyes as she continued. "The more I argued with God, the more I knew I had to write the story and send it. It was time to own it: *my* mother/daughter story. It's not the story I wanted, but it is the story I've been given. I made the decision that I would write it without pretending or even protest; I would write it because it's the only one I have to write.

"So, I got back to the house, literally crawled over my dresser to get to my computer, sat in my chair, and began to write. I wrote the truth. It was pretty raw. But mostly just really, really sad. They only wanted two thousand words . . . thank God!

"As I finished, it struck me as so appropriate to be writing this story in the middle of the chaos and mess of my bedroom. That's what I was writing about . . . chaos and mess. I entitled it 'Unfinished.' That was the most hopeful title I could come up with. I wasn't going to tie it up all nicely with a bow . . . that wouldn't be honest. Or forecast some miracle I've yet to see or even imagine. But I do know that it is unfinished, and somehow that feels hopeful. I took some time to edit, but copy editors generally don't let themselves make many mistakes, so I put it in an envelope, addressed it, stamped it (though the thought did occur to me that no stamp might make a good sabotage!), and walked to the corner mailbox before I could change my mind. Then I finished painting my room, crying the whole time.

"I don't think there's even a chance they will publish it. But it was so healing to get it on paper. Published or not, telling my story, even to myself, was healing."

Woman With the Hemorrhage

The story of the woman with the hemorrhage is an intricately woven story. It is the story of the twofold healing of one woman that is set right in the middle of the story of the healing of a daughter. Because of that complexity, we will first read the whole, then reference parts as we reflect on the story.

Now when Jesus returned, a crowd welcomed him, for they were all expecting him. Then a man named Jairus, a synagogue leader, came and fell at Jesus' feet, pleading with him to come to his house because his only daughter, a girl of about twelve, was dying.

As Jesus was on his way, the crowds almost crushed him. And a woman was there who had been subject to bleeding for twelve years, but no one could heal her. She came up behind him and touched the edge of his cloak, and immediately her bleeding stopped.

"Who touched me?" Jesus asked.

When they all denied it, Peter said, "Master, the people are crowding and pressing against you."

But Jesus said, "Someone touched me; I know that power has gone out from me."

Then the woman, seeing that she could not go unnoticed, came trembling and fell at his feet. In the presence of all the people, she told why she had touched him and how she had been instantly healed. Then he said to her, "Daughter, your faith has healed you. Go in peace."

While Jesus was still speaking, someone came from the house of Jairus, the synagogue leader. "Your daughter is dead," he said. "Don't bother the teacher anymore."

Hearing this, Jesus said to Jairus, "Don't be afraid; just believe, and she will be healed."

When he arrived at the house of Jairus, he did not let anyone go in with him except Peter, John and James, and the child's father and mother. Meanwhile, all the people were wailing and mourning for her. "Stop wailing," Jesus said. "She is not dead but asleep."

They laughed at him, knowing that she was dead. But he took her by the hand and said, "My child, get up!" Her spirit returned, and at once she stood up. Then Jesus told them to give her something to eat. Her parents were astonished, but he ordered them not to tell anyone what had happened. (Luke 8:40–56)

A Continual Confession

And a woman was there who had been subject to bleeding for twelve years. (Luke 8:43)

Self-confessions are powerful words. Those are the things we say about ourselves to ourselves and to others. Most of the time, they operate on an automatic, unthinking basis, below the waterline of consciousness, formed more through subconscious habit than thoughtful intention. Many times they are negative. Often we dismiss them as unimportant. We are sadly mistaken.

The woman with the hemorrhage had a community-dictated self-confession: unclean. Due to her continual bleeding, she was required to warn those around her that she was unclean according to Jewish ceremonial law lest they also become unclean through accidentally touching her.

I sat for a few minutes the other day and just let that imagined reality sink in. "Unclean." The first word of every conversation. I pictured her going through the narrow cobblestone streets. "Unclean, unclean." Her introduction to every stranger. I pictured her at the well or at an open market, the children and adults whispering, "Unclean." Proof that her touch held potential danger, inconvenience at best. The stares and turned shoulders. Unclean. A predetermined, always justified reason for rejection. How many times did she say it in a day? A few minutes of imagining her reality was all I could stand.

That which we say repetitively becomes a part of who we are. Even if it is a message given to us by others. Even if it's untrue. Listen for a while to your own self-confessions. If you are like many women, the brutality and self-deprecation will make your skin crawl. In response to forgetting to bring cookies for your child's class party: "You are so stupid." In response to forgetting to turn off the oven: "Disaster. You are such a disaster." In response to being overweight, it matters not how little or how much: "What a slob." In response to an untidy room: "You are such a pig." In response to an unfinished to-do list: "Lazy." After enjoying even a reasonable portion of a tasty dessert: "Glutton!" In response to relational confusion, often borne out of mixed messages from others: "You are crazy!" In response to needing time to process or learn new skills: "Pea brain!" The truer self-confession is one that says our self-confessions are usually way too brutal.

Without an Advocate?

The way the writer set this story within another story raises questions about connections between the two. This woman had been bleeding for twelve years; the child was twelve years old. Interestingly, Jesus eventually refers to the woman as "Daughter."

But the aspect that most intrigues me is the difference between the daughter having an advocate and the woman having none. In many places in Scripture, we see family members or friends seeking healing for their kin. This woman apparently had no one. None, that is, except herself.

Learning to be our own advocate is a very painful and difficult journey for many women and often not one we undertake unless all else fails. There is something within us that wants to be rescued by another, like the little girl was by her brave father. There is something that tempts us to believe that we are inherently flawed if we do not have an advocate other than ourselves.

As much as we might want it, we do not all get that kind of story. We will not always have others to plead our cause and work for our good. That may be sad, but it is not shameful. It is a reality, but not a commentary on our worth. When we don't have another to advocate for us, God calls it *faith*, not *failure*, our salvation, not our shame to become our own advocate.

Breaking the Rules

She came up behind him and touched the edge of his cloak, and immediately her bleeding stopped. (Luke 8:44)

The Jewish law was clear: If you were unclean, you could not touch another. It was against the law. Some say that even to be in a crowd, much less a pressing crowd, was also a violation. The risk of touching another was too great.

We know she'd made every other effort she could imagine . . . twelve years' worth. Had she broken the law before? We don't know. She probably did in this moment. Maybe she was used to operating "under the radar." She seemed to successfully pull it off. If it weren't for Jesus' divine knowing, she'd have gotten her healing and been free and clear.

A friend recently gave me a mug with the saying *Well-behaved women rarely make history*. The most interesting thing about that sentiment is that it's so biblical! Note the women in Jesus' own genealogy: Ruth, Bathsheba, Rahab, and Tamar. All were women involved in questionable ethical situations. All were women who made the choice for life; all made history. Just like this woman.

I met recently with a woman who was almost giddy with delight over the healing God was bringing into her life through the story of Rahab. "She lied. Rahab lied. And the writer of Hebrews called it faith, and James called her righteous!" The woman who was speaking is a survivor of unimaginable childhood sexual abuse, perpetrated by her father, who also happened to be a preacher with much respect in the small community in which she lived. She had been seeking some theological resolution to the childhood guilt she felt for disobeying her father when she reported the abuse.

Her freedom came as she grasped God's affirmation of Rahab, another woman who disobeyed our common moral code for the sake of survival and was blessed by God. Though I hesitate to advocate such choices when other options exist, God's ways are not our ways, and we would be dishonest not to at least be willing to observe from the stories of women in Scripture that many of them found healing as they broke, rather than followed, the rules.

Healed, yet Still Wounded

"Who touched me?" Jesus asked.

When they all denied it, Peter said, "Master, the people are crowding and pressing against you."

But Jesus said, "Someone touched me; I know that power has gone out from me." (Luke 8:45–46)

The writer makes sure we know that this woman knew her body was instantly made well. Yet she hid? For the first time in twelve years it was legal for her to be seen in the crowd and touched by others, so what was holding her back? Did she feel like she might be in trouble? Guilty for what she had done? Had she taken a healing that was not hers to take? Would he take it back? *Could* he take it back?

Her hiding and her trembling seem to say that she could not imagine anything good from his question. This woman had possessed the faith to reach for the healing she knew she needed. Likely, she believed that such healing would solve all her problems. But here she is trembling. Was she, like the victim of an evil father's abuse, feeling guilty for choosing to break the rules in order to survive?

One common form of self-sabotage I observe in my own life and with many women is an overwhelming feeling of shame after a moment of goodness and shining. Have you ever opened up to a group of women and then kicked yourself around the room on the way home for talking too much, even if the exchange has been healing? Have you ever made a wise remark and convinced yourself before the evening was over that it was shallow or inappropriate? Have you ever dared to weep with a friend and then called it "silly blubbering"? So often we share this woman's experience of being healed, yet still feeling wounded.

Trembling, Clueless Faith

Then the woman, seeing that she could not go unnoticed, came trembling and fell at his feet. In the presence of all the people, she told why she had touched him and how she had been instantly healed. (Luke 8:47)

The woman with the hemorrhage likely didn't know a lot about this rabbi. She had concluded that his reputation as a healer made it worth the risk of the crowd. Her plan had worked; she was healed. She knew why she came; she knew what had happened. But she had no clue about what was happening now.

When Jesus stopped and called her forth, she did not come forward willingly. She came only because she was convinced that she could not go unnoticed. She did not come in courage; she was trembling. All she had was her honest story. Facing the One who knew that power had gone out from him when she touched the hem of his outer garment, what good would a spin game be? There was no point in pretense. She came and told her story.

Faith That Heals, or the Slippery Slope?

Then he said to her, "Daughter, your faith has healed you. Go in peace." (Luke 8:48)

In case you haven't yet noticed, this is a radical story. This is a list of the choices that Jesus is saying constitute a healing faith:

She made a conscious choice to break the rules.

She advocated for herself.

She did not see her own need for more healing.

She obeyed only because she felt discovery was unavoidable.

She obeyed in fear and trembling.

It may not have been pretty; but it got the job done! Several old friends (and a few new) and I got together several months ago for a weekend of simply sharing our stories. We were all women serving in some capacity in the church. We brought suggestions for reflection to prompt conversation but no one had predetermined a theme other than to share our stories of the past, present, and maybe the future.

Interestingly, though, a theme emerged: the slippery slope. As our stories collected within our circle, we discovered that we had one thing in common: We had all found new life rather than death at the bottom of what we had been warned was an ominous slippery slope. At some point in our journey, we had left the path of unthinking compliance to unbending rules that were not offering us the life we knew God desired for us. We opened our eyes to see things in new ways and we followed our hearts, hearts that we had been taught to wholly distrust. Those choices ended up among the most blessed, faith-filled choices we had ever made, producing abundant good fruit of *"love, joy, peace, patience, kindness, goodness, faithfulness, gentleness, self-control"* (Galatians 5:22–23 NASB).

The slippery slope was different for each one. For some it meant reading the writings of feminist theologians. For one, acknowledging the wisdom she had learned in her garden as God's revelation through creation. For another, it was worshiping for a season with a Jewish community, experiencing her roots. One woman went to seminary. Another read widely and quoted secular authors. One woman went to massage school. Another took a wine tour on her last vacation. All had been warned they were on a slippery slope. While they did not dismiss or disrespect such warnings, they also knew and considered a larger work of God at play within and around them, and proceeded with wise and listening hearts.

Now, I would not dare to suggest that all slippery slopes lead to good places; clearly life holds real temptation and very real danger, physical as well as emotional and spiritual hazards. But in light of stories like this one in Scripture and from our collective lives, I think it is also wise to note that sometimes we find a rich and verdant valley of healing faith at the bottom of what we were told was a dangerous slippery slope.

The Stewardship of Stories

Have you ever considered how much power Jesus invested in our stories when he said *"You will be my witnesses"* (Acts 1:8)? The church gathers—one conversation at a time—around stories. No one is optional or not needed. It is only through the gathering of these stories that we come to see the work and presence of God. When we allow pain and shame to sabotage and silence our storytelling, much is lost.

The psalmist says, *"He made known his ways to Moses, his deeds to the people of Israel"* (Psalm 103:7). God's deeds are singular events or snapshots of God at work; God's ways are a collective view, allowing both a deeper and broader understanding of God. In Scripture, God has given us more story than law or precept. I see that as an invitation to listen to the collective as Moses did. Our stories, both then and now, hold wisdom not quickly mined. As we speak our stories in concert with those of old, God invites us not to settle for knowing his deeds, but to seek to listen long and deep, to know God himself.

Lori (continued)

Part of our routine at our women's story circle was to check in with one another as we began. Sometimes someone had an issue that needed our attention before the work of the evening began. That was the case about two months after Lori first told the story of her mother/daughter magazine submission.

"I don't believe it!" Lori began. "They accepted my story. [Wild whoops and hollers of congratulations!] They're going to publish it in the mother/daughter issue. I have the letter here.

"I really didn't think it was important to me whether they published it or not. And in a way, it wasn't. . . . Just writing it was gift enough. But it means so much to have them hear it, really hear it, and, I guess, bless it by publishing it. They saw my story as worthy of being told. True and noble and good even if it lacks beauty or completion or refinement or even being the way I really want it to be. There's something in me that feels more whole, I think. It feels good, really good."

The group affirmed Lori's courage and sought to help her see how much her own faith had to do with her new healing. She gratefully received our words with a tearstained and radiant face.

Your Story

1. Thinking back on your day, what self-confessions have swirled around in your head? What have you said out loud to yourself or others today about yourself? Keep track of both this week.
2. Tell a story of when you, like Jairus's daughter, were the beneficiary of an effective and loving advocate. How did you feel?
3. Tell a story of when you advocated for yourself. How did you feel?
4. Have you ever broken a rule and seen a positive result? Did you feel guilty or ashamed? How did you deal with your feelings?
5. Have you ever felt shame for being in pain? Tell the story.

6. Is there a particular story that has come to mind this week, one that needs to be told, trembling and all?
7. What slippery slopes have you negotiated in your time? What did you find at the bottom?
8. Do you, like Lori, have an unfinished story that you have not told because it is not lovely or complete? Find a safe friend this week and dare to acknowledge and bless your story as you speak it.

10

Choosing to Re-Create
in the Midst of Loss

Letting Go

It is time to go.
I can smell it,
Breathe it
Touch it.
And something in me
Trembles.
I cannot cry,
Only sit bewildered,
Brave and helpless,
That it is time.

Time to go.
Time to step out
Of the world
I shaped
And watched become.
Time to let go

Of the status
And the admiration.

Time to go.
To turn my back
On a life that throbs
With my vigor
And a spirit
That soared
Through my tears.

Time to go
From all that I am
To all that I have
Not yet become.

I cannot cry,
But tremble
At the death
Within me,
And sob—
Tearless—
At the grief
That heaves
My soul.

Time to go.
Lonely,
Brave departure
That stands
Erect and smiling
Whilst my very being
Shudders
In utter nakedness.[1]

EDWINA GATELEY

CONSIDER: Name any losses, large or small, that you have experienced within the last twelve months.

Ann

Of all the different things I do within the umbrella of ministry, my favorite is spiritual formation retreats for small groups of women. I met Ann on one such outing. She and her co-workers came on retreat as they were dealing with a shift in management. The entire team was angry, disillusioned, and literally on the verge of tendering their resignations.

Ann arrived with a relatively narrow list of questions: Can I salvage my job (and my sanity) by learning to cope with the situation, or is resignation necessary?

One of the opening exercises was to choose an art card that best reflected where they were at this moment of arrival. Ann selected a very busy-looking, almost chaotic Salvador Dali image. It had mostly muted colors, a washed-out palette in black and beige. When I asked the women to introduce themselves using their cards, Ann's tears began.

"I think this card is horrible. Is my life really like this? I know it is because I picked this card with that in mind, but I guess I've never really looked at my own reality until now. How did I ever get here? Has this job done this to me in just nine months? My marriage is not on the rocks, and as far as I know, my kids aren't on drugs. I'm working for a Christian ministry, for goodness' sake! This is what I had always dreamed about doing! You'd think it would all be good; not like *this*.

"And anger. I see anger in this card. I've never been this angry before. How is it that all this work stuff makes me so mad? I hate being like this," Ann asserted, with her voice melting and tears forming again. Ann was asking some good questions. She was also overwhelmed by her own deep emotion accompanying the profound realization that the current state of her life was not at all how she wanted to live. Maybe it wasn't all about the new leadership.

"That's what this time is all about," I offered, seeking to ease some of Ann's anxiety. "We're going to try to get a handle on where we are and what brought us to this place. Then we'll look at some ways to live differently and maybe what new thing God might be doing. There may also be things we might need to let go. I know it is unpleasant, but it is also an odd grace to begin this retreat with such a profound realization that you are not where you want to be."

"Well, I've got that one down then," she said, wiping her tears with a little laugh.

As we continued with the work of the retreat, more pieces of Ann's story surfaced. After many years at home with her children, she had returned to the workplace in a high-profile job about nine months earlier. With an hour and a half commute each way, her days were long and she was physically exhausted.

Another part of her struggle was because she had had four different bosses in those nine months. Such major shifts in leadership kept her workplace context unpredictable and her energy given to adjusting rather than creating. Ann was spent on every level.

Though all those issues added to her burden, it wasn't until we made collages on the second day of our retreat that Ann's deeper soul ache began to surface. By this time, Ann was more rested and had off-loaded some of the immediately brimming emotional pain she had brought.

After studying Hannah's story and the critically important naming process that she had experienced (see chapter 8 of this book), I asked the women to make a collage that communicated something of their true selves, who they were and who they were not. Though the retreatants were initially reluctant, the fifty pounds worth of various magazines and collage materials (ribbon, old jewelry, silk flowers, paints, markers, and a very odd collection of this and that) that I had carted two thousand miles began to inspire them. As soft music played and I walked among the prayerful women, I heard many sighs and groans of new insight being birthed.

After an hour of work, their reluctant beginning concluded with an equally reluctant end. We took a short break and decided to reassemble outside. We gathered the lawn chairs in a circle in view of the beautiful lake that surrounded the home where we were staying. Ann went first.

As she showed us her design, I was immediately struck by how different it was from the card she had chosen the day before. Ann's small piece of poster board was covered edge to edge, and even beyond the edge, with verdant green. It had four quadrants, much like an English garden with hedges. Each quadrant was filled with colors—bright, saturated, and rich. She bubbled and giggled with laughter as she explained each section. Then unexpectedly, her emotion shifted.

"This is me. This is the *real* me," Ann began with a strong and utterly grounded voice. Then in a tearful whisper she continued, "So why is the life I am living right now so *not* this? So not *me*?"

Naomi

Idyllic to Empty

Her name meant "pleasant," and it was a fitting name for Naomi. As we meet her in Ruth 1, we learn that she had a husband and two sons. *Two* sons. A Jewish woman of Naomi's time with two sons likely considered herself to be fortunate indeed. She also had a brave, provisionary husband who moved his family to Moab when the food supply in Israel ran low.

Naomi may well have been living the dream she'd imagined for herself. Her vision was rooted in her rich heritage and cultural identity connecting a woman's significance and life worth to her children, chiefly sons. So it is no wonder she felt completely empty when her husband and both sons died.

Now Elimelek, Naomi's husband, died, and she was left with her two sons. They married Moabite women, one named Orpah and the other Ruth. After they had lived there about ten years, both Mahlon and Kilion also died, and Naomi was left without her two sons and her husband. (Ruth 1:3–5)

Naomi's wonderful life unraveled. Loss comes to all our lives, in one form or another, sometimes expected and sometimes unexpected. Certainly though, few of us experience loss in the extreme way that Naomi did. Yet it is that very extremity that helps us see more clearly the path this wise woman took toward healing, how she masterfully entered her grief, allowing her life to be re-created in the midst of loss rather than sabotaging the remainder of her life through trying to avoid her overwhelming pain.

The Pull of Home

When Naomi heard in Moab that the Lord had come to the aid of his people by providing food for them, she and her daughters-in-law prepared to return home from there. With her two daughters-in-law she left the place where she had been living and set out on the road that would take them back to the land of Judah. (Ruth 1:6–7)

Most of us have experienced the draw of home in hard times. We want to crawl under the covers and be cared for by others. We want to be surrounded by the familiar. In some ways, we want to return to the womb.

When Naomi heard that there was food at home, she made the bold decision to return. Such a choice feels unusually brave given that her social and economic status was likely very low as a widow without children. It had been at least ten years since she had been in Bethlehem. Much had happened in that time, both in the city and within her own life. That's often where our longing for home gets tricky. We want to return to the womb, but we have grown beyond it. Like it or not, life has changed us.

Letting Go

Then Naomi said to her two daughters-in-law, "Go back, each of you, to your mother's home. May the Lord show you kindness, as you have shown kindness to your dead husbands and to me. May the Lord grant that each of you will find rest in the home of another husband."

Then she kissed them goodbye and they wept aloud and said to her, "We will go back with you to your people."

But Naomi said, "Return home, my daughters. Why would you come with me? Am I going to have any more sons, who could become your husbands? Return home, my daughters; I am too old to have another husband. Even if I thought there was still hope for me—even if I had a husband tonight and then gave birth to sons—would you wait until they grew up? Would you remain unmarried for them? No, my daughters. It is more bitter for me than for you, because the Lord's hand has turned against me!" (Ruth 1:8–13)

As Naomi left, she encouraged her daughters-in-law to stay in Moab. All the hopes and dreams of future generations that would have originally bound these women together felt forever lost. Naomi obviously deeply loved Ruth and Orpah, but could no longer afford to care for them on any level. In distancing herself from them, Naomi may have thought that she was seeking their good as well as her own. She was hurt and angry. She felt that God himself was against her.

As she left Moab, Naomi saw her life as a blank slate, without hope or a future. She told her daughters-in-law, *"Why would you come with me?"* and spelled out her hopelessness for them. All she saw before her was bitterness and continuing opposition from God. Though some might label her overt discouragement as unhealthy depression, it sounds to me like a woman who is grieving well: she is entering fully into her loss in an unguarded way, choosing a difficult but ultimately healing path. She is letting her old life disintegrate, letting it go in a way that will, in time, open her to new life.

Pain That Blinds

At this they wept aloud again. Then Orpah kissed her mother-in-law goodbye, but Ruth clung to her.

"Look," said Naomi, "your sister-in-law is going back to her people and her gods. Go back with her."

> *But Ruth replied, "Don't urge me to leave you or to turn*
> *back from you. Where you go I will go, and where you stay*
> *I will stay. Your people will be my people and your God my*
> *God. Where you die I will die, and there I will be buried.*
> *May the Lord deal with me, be it ever so severely, if even*
> *death separates you and me." When Naomi realized that*
> *Ruth was determined to go with her, she stopped urging her.*
> *(Ruth 1:14–18)*

Pain upon pain. Everyone was in tears. The women experienced intense hurt in the tearing away. So much so, perhaps, that Ruth determined she simply would not leave. She approached her mother-in-law with a force of will stronger than Naomi's.

Naomi acquiesced, perhaps because she did not have the strength to resist. She certainly had no vision for goodness or light or hope. Interestingly, she openly dismissed the two things God eventually used to turn this story around: Ruth and the Jewish custom that allowed a young widow to marry a relative of the deceased man and produce children in the dead man's name to allow that lineage to continue (vv. 12–13). Naomi's pain had blinded her to any possibility of the redemptive and healing work of God—the very work that had already begun in her life through Ruth's insistence.

As we enter into our grief in times of loss, such a narrowing of vision is unavoidable and not something God judges or moves to correct. Naomi's inability to see did not inhibit the ongoing work of God. One of the messages of this story is that God is actively creating good, in and around and through our seasons of painful disillusionment, quite apart from our vision or energies or efforts. As we give ourselves to the process of letting go of old and beautiful ideas about our lives,

God is busy creating a new, beyond-our-imagination future. Yet even the wisest cannot see it in the moment.

A New Name

So the two women went on until they came to Bethlehem. When they arrived in Bethlehem, the whole town was stirred because of them, and the women exclaimed, "Can this be Naomi?"

"Don't call me Naomi," she told them. "Call me Mara, because the Almighty has made my life very bitter." (Ruth 1:19–20)

Grief changes the core of our being. Naomi was wise enough to know that. So when she arrived home and those who knew her the best almost did not recognize her, she decided that her name no longer fit. *Pleasant* would not work; so she adopted the name *Mara,* meaning "bitter."

Interestingly, we have no reference to anyone, the narrator included, who ever used the alternate name. For some women of our day, renaming themselves can be a way of distancing themselves from the grief and loss of divorce or widowhood. For Naomi, it was a way of acknowledging her grief more powerfully, intimately integrating it into her life and personhood. Wisdom invites us to enfold our loss into our identity, to be re-formed by it, re-shaped by it, re-created by it.

Owning Emptiness

I went away full, but the Lord has brought me back empty. Why call me Naomi? The Lord has afflicted me; the Almighty has brought misfortune upon me. (Ruth 1:21)

When we grieve well, as Naomi did, sooner or later, we find ourselves at a place of utter emptiness. It is, for many, that place of greatest pain. This emptiness is not simply a static void but a dry, lifeless hole that seems to actively suck all potential for life into its darkness. In these moments, much like Naomi, we experience gross disorientation. All we have known about our future, ourselves, and our God, the very bedrock of our lives, has given way under our feet. Our lives fall apart.

It is challenging to find anyone willing to abide in the presence of such pain, even those who are experiencing it, much less an observer. Most of us have a strong and grief-sabotaging drive to escape. We try to fill the hole so we will not feel it. We stuff ourselves with busyness, noise, food, drink, new purchases, and fun. But resisting the reality or experience of the pain and chaos does not serve us well; it often prolongs our suffering.

Grief to Gratitude

Her mother-in-law asked her, "Where did you glean today? Where did you work? Blessed be the man who took notice of you!"

Then Ruth told her mother-in-law about the one at whose place she had been working. "The name of the man I worked with today is Boaz," she said.

"The Lord bless him!" Naomi said to her daughter-in-law. "He has not stopped showing his kindness to the living and the dead." She added, "That man is our close relative; he is one of our guardian-redeemers" (Ruth 2:19–20).

I just love the way Eugene Peterson translates verse 20 in *The Message*. (Though I know it is an overtly cultural projection, I hear Naomi's words with a southern twang!)

Naomi said to her daughter-in-law, "Why, God bless that man! God hasn't quite walked out on us after all! He still loves us, in bad times as well as good!" (Ruth 2:20 THE MESSAGE)

When we are faithful to know and live the depths of our grief and the profound ache of emptiness, we will, in time, find our hurting souls to be the good soil into which God plants seeds of hope. This is one such moment of hope.

This sudden shift in Naomi, from grief to gratitude, was the direct fruit of laboring well through her grief. Many an obstetrician's lunch has been spoiled by a woman who has labored with birth pangs for hours with little discernible progress only to suddenly find the baby ready to be born. This shift in Naomi's life seems quick only because she had not sabotaged and resisted the ongoing, incredibly profound pain that had softened her heart.

We think our grief will kill us, so we resist entering the depths of its pain. We assume that it is destructive rather than productive. However, much like birth pangs, if we will relax into grief, it will hurt less and bring us closer and closer to the new life we so long to experience. Ironically, it is the *resistance* of such pain not the experience of it that sabotages our growth and prolongs the process.

Gratitude to Re-Creation

At our church not long ago, I visited with a middle-aged widow who had lost her husband almost three years ago and was faithfully grieving his death. When I asked if she would ever consider remarriage, she very quickly, very definitively, and somewhat harshly snapped, "No. Never!"

Though she could well articulate the goodness of God in the midst of grief, she could not yet tolerate the thought of new visions of a meaningful future that did not include her husband. She could not yet think about the re-creation of her life beyond the reach of her grief for him. It wasn't so much what she said that told me that, but how she said it—reflexively not reflectively. Though, of course, remarriage may or may not be in her future, my hope is that at some point in her grief journey she will dare to be open to re-creation.

As Ruth chapter 3 begins, Naomi is ready to re-create her life. She focuses her creative energy on a plot to secure her daughter-in-law's future. Her blindness has lifted and she can see that her life is not so empty after all. She works with what she has—in this case, Ruth and marriage customs.

One day Ruth's mother-in-law Naomi said to her, "My daugh-ter, I must find a home for you, where you will be well pro-vided for. Now Boaz, with whose women you have worked, is a relative of ours. Tonight he will be winnowing barley on the threshing floor. Wash, put on perfume, and get dressed in your best clothes. Then go down to the threshing floor, but don't let him know you are there until he has finished eating and drinking. When he lies down, note the place where he is lying. Then go and uncover his feet and lie down. He will tell you what to do." (Ruth 3:1–4)

Renewed Life . . . Far Beyond Her Imagination

All went according to Naomi's plan: Boaz proposed, and married Ruth, who bore an heir for Naomi. Though the au-thor told this story heretofore as the suffering and healing tale of two simple peasant women, we discover now that they were ancestors of King David.

So Boaz took Ruth and she became his wife. When he made love to her, the Lord enabled her to conceive, and she gave birth to a son. The women said to Naomi: "Praise be to the Lord, who this day has not left you without a guardian-redeemer. May he become famous throughout Israel! He will renew your life and sustain you in your old age. For your daughter-in-law, who loves you and who is better to you than seven sons, has given him birth."

Then Naomi took the child in her arms and cared for him. The women living there said, "Naomi has a son!" And they named him Obed. He was the father of Jesse, the father of David. (Ruth 4:13–17)

The unseen hand of God was always at work in the healing of Naomi's life. Refusing to allow her profound loss to sabotage the remainder of her life, Naomi's grief work became the soil in which God planted new seeds of new dreams. In the end, God went way beyond Naomi's imagination in blessing her with a grandson and generations beyond. Who knows what God may do for us when we, too, dare to re-create our lives after loss!

Ann (continued)

As Ann stood in our small circle of lawn chairs that day, in healing tears, she began to face and feel the emptiness of her life. Having fashioned an image of the verdant green life she knew she was created to live, she began to ask new questions about her current life experience. The gap between her fragmented and barren reality and her verdant green vision prompted new questions, chief among them: What had caused such emptiness, and how had loss come about without her noticing?

Over the next day, Ann began to uncover a startlingly large number of un-grieved losses that had intersected her life, all within the last two years. Her mother's Alzheimer's condition had deteriorated so rapidly that she had been moved to a nursing home. Not only was Ann losing her mother, she was also losing hope for healing the painful relationship between them. At the same time, Ann's oldest daughter had left the previous fall for college in another state but had struggled to transition, returning home mid-semester.

Additionally, her son had been diagnosed with a learning disability and had to change schools to get the assistance he needed. Also within the last two years, her mother-in-law's mental illness had become so severe that Ann's home was continually disrupted by her interference. Since Ann's husband was her only son, he was struggling with how to care for his mother as well as his own wife and children. The discord had caused so much tension that Ann and her husband were both in counseling. Ann was stunned to discover that every major relationship in her life, and even her sense of safety in her own home, had suffered significantly in the last two years. Though she had worked hard to *manage* each loss, she had failed to truly face them or feel them.

At her workplace, in addition to the series of losses over shifting bosses, she had become generally disillusioned with that Christian institution. The politics were thick and often unjust. She felt she had been intentionally shut out of many professional meetings simply because she was a woman. When she did have an opportunity to share her thoughts, it was as if she were talking to the air. Her long-held vision for meaningful contribution to this ministry was fading fast.

Like so many of us, Ann carried a very heavy load of unrecognized accumulated losses. Each individual issue at the time seemed small and ordinary, so Ann simply pushed through, becoming increasingly burdened by a heavier and heavier load. She also kept a tight lid on her emotions, convinced that if she went there she would never stop crying. Chronic busyness became her coconspirator, with the rushed pace of her life keeping the deeper hurts from surfacing. Somewhere along the way, she had begun to operate on autopilot. Her life had lost all its color. By managing and carrying rather than grieving her losses, the "Ann of the green," who had resurfaced in her collage, slowly became the black and beige chaos of the Salvador Dali art card she had chosen at the beginning of the retreat.

Ann had a bucket of tears to shed, but contrary to what she had expected, she stopped crying that weekend. The emptiness she discovered as she grieved her losses and let go of the old versions and visions of her life felt both painful and freeing. In the lightness of the release, she tasted moments of unexpected laughter that came from deep within. Unlike Naomi's story, Ann's tale of re-creation was yet to be written, but the long-delayed, critically important grief work had finally begun. Ann felt she had already found a few seeds of hope and new life in the collage she created. In the midst of her faithful and painful labor, "Ann of the green" was being reborn.

Your *Story*

1. Take a second look at your list of losses. Having listened to Ann's story, do you have anything to add?
2. How have you handled your losses? What have you done to process them? Do you sense any lingering pain or heaviness around any in particular?
3. Think about those in your life who have known grief. How have they dealt with it? Do their stories resemble Naomi's or conflict with her example? Which do you connect with the most?
4. Have you, like Naomi, ever felt empty? Has your life ever "fallen apart"? Write/tell the story. What did you do? How did you *fill* the space? How did you choose to *feel* it?
5. Can you recall a time when personal pain blinded you to the love of others or the love of God?
6. Recall a moment of re-creating after a loss. Perhaps the dream was folded into another, like egg whites into cake batter. Did it grow up in some way? Was it unraveled and knit into something new? Or was it resurrected altogether?

11

Choosing to Persevere in the Midst of Injustice

By the rivers of Babylon
we sat weeping,
remembering Zion.
There on the poplars
we hung our harps.

Our captors shouted
for happy songs,
for songs of festival.
"Sing!" they cried,
"the songs of Zion."

How could we sing
the song of the Lord
in a foreign land?

Jerusalem forgotten?
Wither my hand!
Jerusalem forgotten?

Silence my voice!
if I do not seek you
as my greatest joy.[1]

PSALM 137:1–6

CONSIDER: Recall a moment when you suffered an injustice. It might have been as simple as someone pulling in front of you in traffic or as heartrending as a custody battle over children. How did you feel? What did you do?

Pauline

Pauline was crying before she even sat down on my sofa. When she found her voice again, she said, "I have been trying to call you for months to make this appointment. But I wanted to wait until I could talk about all this without doing *this* (pointing to her tears)." She smiled and continued, "As you can see, I finally gave up and made the call."

Pauline was an elegant woman in her late fifties. A divorcée of many years and recently retired art teacher, she had deep roots in our community. I was aware that her church had been through some rough times of late and wondered if that pain was the reason for her tears. I knew Pauline only casually before our first spiritual direction appointment, but had a sincere respect for both her spiritual depth and her artistic talents. To be frank, I wondered if there was really anything I could offer her! As I witnessed her sadness, I knew I could at least share her pain.

As the tears slowed, Pauline began, "It's been months, and still the pain is so real for so many. I don't know how much you know about what has gone on downtown," Pauline stated, referencing her church.

"Very little," I replied. "Clearly, you have been in a great deal of pain. I'm glad you decided not to wait any longer to call."

"Me, too. Especially since I now realize I can cry *and* talk," Pauline said. Then her light banter melted into more sobs.

Pauline smiled, taking another tissue. Over the next hour, we talked more about her tears and what they might be saying than about the particulars of the pain that caused them. Knowing her spiritual depth, I offered the possibility that they might be a reflection of the heart of God, intended as a gift from him for the good of her church body.

She asked curiously, "You mean maybe I don't need to work so hard to hide them while I'm in church?"

"Maybe not," I offered. "Do you feel safe enough there to express them? Sometimes the public expression of grief can bring transformation. Are there others in pain besides you?"

"Oh yes. I know from conversations I have had that so many people are still hurting. I guess it follows then that God would be hurting, too, doesn't it?" Pauline said, thinking out loud.

Over the coming months, we explored some of Pauline's other emotional responses to the recent events at her church. We talked a lot about injustice and disillusionment, both integral parts of many church splits. As a longtime member, Pauline had good friends on both sides of the issues and hurt for them all.

She came in one day a few months later more angry than I had seen her before. "I think I just may be going crazy. I can't believe it. I heard this morning that the board has already hired a new preacher." Pauline sat on the edge of her chair, erect and alert; her eyes and words were sharp.

"It's all so unjust! Because they won, they think God's on their side and that they can ignore all these people who hurt. Don't they *care* about the people who used to be their friends? Are they blind? Or is it me? Maybe I'm just a crazy old woman." Her emotion deflated with her last remark.

"Wouldn't that be nice," I said flatly.

"What?" Pauline replied, so surprised by my remark that she began lowering her shoulders and settling back into her usual seat, confused and curious.

"Wouldn't it be nice if all this that we've been talking about for all these months were just the wild imaginings of a crazy old woman? Wouldn't it be nice if all the pain you've felt and the injustices you have witnessed were not real? That these people whom you loved had not really disappointed you? And hurt the *other* people you love so much? We'd both love that," I continued.

"All right. All right," she consented. "So I'm not crazy. But I sure feel like I am when I go to church." Pauline was quick to pick up on the fact that dismissing herself as a crazy old woman was an attempt to sabotage her calling to meet, persevere with, and perhaps even address the injustice before her.

I continued, "Say more about what you feel when you go to church. Is there a sense of pretense or a polite veneer? Could it be that you feel trapped in this web of sorts, a pattern among the leadership of what looks to be determined injustice? A church system doing 'kingdom work' and at the same time ignoring the reality of people in pain? And you see no way out?" I proffered.

"I think you're pretty close," Pauline said in a very discouraged tone.

"That sounds more painful than crazy to me. Now, I know on one hand, you were only kidding by calling yourself crazy. But on the other hand, sometimes even when we're kidding, if we say something enough, we and other people begin to believe it. It could sabotage your ability to help. For sure it cuts down on any imagination about how God might be at work here," I said.

"I hear what you're saying. I've been telling myself that all this week—that I am a crazy old woman. Actually, I would alternate 'crazy' and 'whiney.' It's definitely not getting me anywhere good," she replied with a laugh, quickly discerning her own internal dynamics. After a moment, though, her face grew sad again. "It feels so hopeless though. Like a dead end."

Tamar

Noble Woman

There are only four women mentioned in Jesus' genealogy in Matthew 1: Rahab, Tamar, Ruth, and the wife of Uriah (Bathsheba). All four were women who chose life in the midst of crazy, ethically questionable circumstances. I see their inclusion there as an affirmation of their courageous choices. Tamar's story is likely the least well known.

In order to comprehend her story, it is important to understand a particular Jewish marriage custom. Descendants were so important that if a man died before producing one, his wife was "given" to his brother in order to produce an heir in the dead man's name. It was the noble and honorable custom of the time. However, clearly not everyone liked it or cooperated with the plan.

> *Judah got a wife for Er, his firstborn, and her name was Tamar. But Er, Judah's firstborn, was wicked in the Lord's sight; so the Lord put him to death.*
>
> *Then Judah said to Onan, "Sleep with your brother's wife and fulfill your duty to her as a brother-in-law to raise up offspring for your brother." But Onan knew that the child would not be his; so whenever he slept with his brother's wife, he spilled his semen on the ground to keep from providing offspring for his brother. What he did was wicked in the Lord's sight; so the Lord put him to death also. (Genesis 38:6–10)*

It is difficult to wrestle with the idea of God killing folks, men or women, as punishment for sin. It is interesting, though, to think about the death of these two sons as God's protection for Tamar. Tamar was noble; her husbands, however, were not. She likely had no choice in the selection of a mate, or the recourse of divorce. Who knows what she may have suffered under the hand of these men whom God saw as so evil that he put them to death. It is a frightening thought.

Blaming the Victim

> *Judah then said to his daughter-in-law Tamar, "Live as a widow in your father's household until my son Shelah grows up." For he thought, "He may die too, just like his brothers." (Genesis 38:11)*

As is true of many women who suffer injustice, the victim ends up being blamed for the sin of another. I spoke with a woman the other day who was being told her husband's alcohol addiction was her fault. Another woman's husband yelled at *her* when she caught him secretly studying a Victoria's Secret catalogue (not for the purpose of ordering her lingerie). He told her she shouldn't have left it in the kitchen trash where he would be tempted, that it was her responsibility to take it to the outside garbage. *What?!*

Women are often all too quick to accept the blame for the wrongdoing of others. Though it seems counterintuitive, we actually *prefer* to be to blame. Think about it: When we are at fault, we are still in control. We would *love* to believe that we can whip ourselves into shape and therefore guarantee that this kind of disappointment, pain, and betrayal will never happen again. Sadly, our strategy simply doesn't work. In fact, our acceptance of blame can sabotage or forestall real repentance and change on the part of another, continuing the cycle of sin or abuse. Sometimes we, like Tamar, are truly victims. That, my friends, is a hard but accurate truth.

Tragically, Judah did not seem to question the behavior of his evil sons at all; he had decided that the problem was Tamar. On top of such an unjust conclusion, he was also not forthright about his plan to protect his third, only remaining, son. Perhaps he knew his position was indefensible.

An Initial Response of Trust

So Tamar went to live in her father's household. (Genesis 38:11)

Like many of us, Tamar appears to trust Judah's stated intentions initially. She complied with his request for her to go back to her family. As relationally sensitive women, most of us are inclined to offer some level of initial trust to others. As a relationship begins, our willingness to trust or not says more about us than the other person. Finding a balance between wisdom and cynicism can be a challenge. We do not want to be naïve or foolish; at the same time, to approach others with the expectation of abuse and mistrust covers potential relationships with a blanket of darkness that can be hard for even the most noble person to overcome.

When we find ourselves in the midst of hurt and betrayal as a result of an initial decision to trust, we are tempted to berate ourselves. It is difficult to remember that for the most part, the choice of some preliminary openness is noble rather than foolish.

Choosing Life

After a long time Judah's wife, the daughter of Shua, died. When Judah had recovered from his grief, he went up to Timnah, to the men who were shearing his sheep, and his friend Hirah the Adullamite went with him.

When Tamar was told, "Your father-in-law is on his way to Timnah to shear his sheep," she took off her widow's clothes, covered herself with a veil to disguise herself, and then sat down at the entrance to Enaim, which is on the road to Timnah. For she saw that, though Shelah had now grown up, she had not been given to him as his wife. (Genesis 38:12–14)

I wonder when it dawned on Tamar that Judah was not going to honor his word to her. Though simply stated in the text here, my guess is that it was far from a simple conclusion for Tamar. It is painful to face the facts, to be willing to become disillusioned with someone we had trusted.

We are inclined to doubt our conclusions about the ill intentions of another—so much so that we rarely come to the point of action that Tamar did in this story. By refusing to acknowledge, meet, and persevere in opposition to injustice, we can sabotage our health and our growth, clinging to idyllic views of those we love despite obvious evidence to the contrary. Naïveté comes in at least two different forms: being too trusting initially *and* being unwilling to change our opinion of reality as new information unfolds. Though denial is sometimes a stage of a healthy grief journey, it can also be evidence of determined foolishness. Denial in this situation would not be faith in the other; it would be foolishness. No amount of positive expectation would have changed Judah's intent.

Disillusionment is the choice to confront the illusion, the lie we once believed—and it is painful. It invites us not only to engage the pain of the disappointment immediately before us but also asks us to grapple with our own misjudgment and vulnerability to future harm. Tamar was not only courageous enough to face the truth of her situation, she was also bold enough to make a plan to work around it.

Creative Solutions

Many times we see injustice as a dead end. We throw up our hands in anger and give up. To acknowledge that we are a victim becomes the end of the story; we conclude that we are utterly helpless. This is another point at which sabotage can catch us. If we cannot have our fairy tale come true, we will just opt out.

Tamar, however, saw the injustice she faced more as a detour than a dead end. Though she was initially a victim of Judah's deception, she did not take on *victim* as an identity. She refused helplessness as a way of life. She was determined to find another way; she was determined to choose *life*. She came up with a creative, and face it, deceptive and ethically questionable solution to the dilemma before her.

> *When Judah saw her, he thought she was a prostitute, for she had covered her face. Not realizing that she was his daughter-in-law, he went over to her by the roadside and said, "Come now, let me sleep with you."*
>
> *"And what will you give me to sleep with you?" she asked.*
>
> *"I'll send you a young goat from my flock," he said.*
>
> *"Will you give me something as a pledge until you send it?" she asked.*
>
> *He said, "What pledge should I give you?"*
>
> *"Your seal and its cord, and the staff in your hand," she answered. So he gave them to her and slept with her, and she became pregnant by him. After she left, she took off her veil and put on her widow's clothes again. (Genesis 38:15–19)*

Judah had no idea who he was messing with, both when he arrogantly refused to send for Tamar once his son was of age *and* when he unknowingly met her on the road! In the first instance, perhaps he still saw her as a child. He likely had no regard at all for the woman he assumed was a prostitute.

Tamar, however, had survived two evil husbands and undoubtedly done some growing up. Judah was dealing with a shrewd woman. Her plan reflects knowledge of her father-in-law's less-than-noble habits. It would not surprise me if she also knew that she was fertile at the time of this encounter. When she tricked Judah, she was careful to make sure she had proof of the encounter. With fertility interpreted as a gift from God, it even looks like God was cooperating with her scheme!

Courageously Confronting Injustice

The writer of this story does little to protect the reputation of Judah. What we know thus far is that he had two very evil sons, he lied to Tamar, and he slept with a prostitute (for all he knew). Oh, but things get *much* worse.

Meanwhile Judah sent the young goat by his friend the Adullamite in order to get his pledge back from the woman, but he did not find her. He asked the men who lived there, "Where is the shrine prostitute who was beside the road at Enaim?"

"There hasn't been any shrine prostitute here," they said.

So he went back to Judah and said, "I didn't find her. Besides, the men who lived there said, 'There hasn't been any shrine prostitute here.' "

Then Judah said, "Let her keep what she has, or we will become a laughingstock. After all, I did send her this young goat, but you didn't find her."

About three months later Judah was told, "Your daughter-in-law Tamar is guilty of prostitution, and as a result she is now pregnant."

Judah said, "Bring her out and have her burned to death!"

As she was being brought out, she sent a message to her father-in-law. "I am pregnant by the man who owns these," she said. And she added, "See if you recognize whose seal and cord and staff these are." (Genesis 38:20–25)

Though Judah made an initial attempt to keep his promise to the prostitute, he was primarily concerned about his reputation and dropped the matter without further investigation when he feared that his indiscretion might be discovered. When he found out Tamar was pregnant, allegedly as a result of prostitution (of which he was also guilty), he called for her to be brought out and publicly burned, baby and all! The hypocrisy and injustice of it is enough to make your blood boil!

Tamar's wisdom and cunning shine in this artfully crafted drama. Interestingly, she did not reveal her "hand," so to speak, until the last minute when she was being brought out to be burned. It appears that Judah was not even present for the gruesome event he had ordered. I wonder if she had hoped for a face-to-face confrontation.

Blessed by Others and God

Many people wrestle with the outcome of this story. Tamar is not only declared "more righteous" by Judah, the sons she bore with Judah were given a place in the kingly lineage of David and Jesus (Matthew 1:3). Go figure!

Judah recognized them and said, "She is more righteous than I, since I wouldn't give her to my son Shelah." And he did not sleep with her again. When the time came for her to give birth, there were twin boys in her womb. (Genesis 38:26–27)

Imagine all the blessings that would have been lost had this courageous woman not persevered in the midst of rank injustice! Admittedly, the situation messes with our categories of goodness, offering us another insight into the manifold grace of God. Tamar's story invites us to persevere, not to allow the detouring forces of injustice to sabotage our calling, our lives, or our creativity!

Pauline (continued)

Pauline did find the courage to let her tears flow in church. They were neither insincere nor contrived. She did not put them on display as a show, but she was willing to grieve with

God in the moment. Some friends began to offer comfort to her and in so doing, they also began to heal. Others were less than supportive.

When we next met, Pauline began, "You know, from the first day we talked about the idea that the tears I wanted to get rid of might actually be a work of God, my soul started to heal. Now even when folks aren't supportive, it's okay. One old friend of mine even came up to me and asked me to 'leave the tissues at home once the new pastor gets here.' *Ugh*. I know he's not an evil person. He just wants the pain to be over. He simply can't see what he can't see."

"God has really grown your compassion, hasn't he?" I noted.

"I guess he has," Pauline agreed. "But if you think that means leaving my tissues at home, think again. If the tears come, they come. They will be shed. But something is changing. I'm beginning to be able to see beyond the tears."

"Say more," I invited.

"Well, I can't instantly take the grief away. Hurting people still seem to be coming out of the woodwork. My guess is that many who haven't come in a while because of the pain will come to see the new pastor. But there is also a part of me that is really, really wanting to celebrate. I don't know what it will look like, but I do know that God is going to resurrect this church. He's been doing that in churches for thousands of years. There's something in me that wants to reach beyond the tears even while I'm still shedding them!"

"You know, one of the things we've talked about is how God often uses artists and poets to speak out against injustice—much the way Tamar did. Is there something you can do with your art?" I wondered aloud.

"I don't know, but it sure gives me another way to think about it all," Pauline said.

The next month Pauline returned with a glowing demeanor. As we exchanged a hug, she sang, "Praise God from whom all blessings flow. Praise him all creatures here below. Praise him above, ye heavenly hosts. Praise Father, Son, and Holy Ghost. Amen."

"Amen," I echoed with growing curiosity.

"That's it! That's the answer to our prayers!" Pauline announced.

"Go on . . ." I said. Now I was the one with the confused and curious smile.

"That's what I've decided to do! I am going to splash the ancient wisdom of the doxology all over our fellowship hall in bold and beautiful banners. Well, not me, actually, but a whole group of us—anyone who wants to come and help. I've already designed them, gotten approval, and found funding, and a friend and I bought the fabric yesterday. Can you believe it?" Pauline's face beamed healing and hope, beauty and vision.

"Pauline, what a *brilliant* idea!" I said in amazement. "And you've gotten all that done in a month's time?"

"It's remarkable, isn't it? I think I had a bit of Wind behind my back," she said with a sly grin. "And you haven't even heard the best part yet. As people are signing up to work on · the banners, I am praying for God to bring them together in just the right small groups. I'm doing as much of it in my home as I can—a neutral location. I am praying fiercely that God will knit us all together as a church while we are creating these banners . . . and collect us around this central truth that unites us all in the first place: praising God! Not bad for a crazy old whiney woman," Pauline said with a grin and a wink.

Your *Story*

1. Recall your response to our opening question. Do you see it any differently in light of Tamar and Pauline's stories? Explain.

2. Have you ever suffered as a victim and been unjustly blamed? Did you accept the blame? Refuse it?

3. Situations of injustice can sometimes leave us feeling as if we are crazy. The psalm that opens this chapter (137) tells of Jewish captives exiled from their homeland being asked to sing the happy song of Jerusalem to their captors. Have you ever been asked to pretend all is well, to "sing happy songs" in the midst of deep pain or injustice?

4. Do you consider yourself to be a wisely trusting person? Tell a story of when you faced painful disillusionment with a previously trusted person.

5. Do you tend to react to injustice as a dead end or as a detour? Give examples of each from your experience.

6. Share what you think and how you feel about Tamar's creative solution. Does it offend you? Delight you? Do you feel both reactions?

7. How do you feel about Judah's proclamation of Tamar as the "more righteous"? Have you ever experienced injustice being turned on its head? Tell your story.

8. Have you ever experienced a church split like Pauline did or another form of institutional injustice? What elements of injustice were involved? How have you dealt with the outcome? How have you dealt honestly with your pain?

12

Choosing to Grow Up

I am becoming the woman I've wanted,
grey at the temples,
soft body, delighted,
cracked up by life
with a laugh that's known bitter
but, past it, got better,
knows she's a survivor—
that whatever comes,
she can outlast it.
I am becoming a deep
weathered basket.

I am becoming the woman I've longed for,
the motherly lover
with arms strong and tender,
the growing up daughter
who blushes surprises.
I am becoming full moons
and sunrises.
I find her becoming,

this woman I've wanted,
who knows she'll encompass,
who knows she's sufficient,
knows where she's going
and travels with passion.
Who remembers she's precious,
but knows she's not scarce—
who knows she is plenty,
plenty to share.[1]

JAYNE RELAFORD BROWN

CONSIDER: Recall and describe a time when you interjected your voice, opinion, or ideas into a situation, large or small, and improved the outcome. Recall a time when you failed to speak up and later regretted your decision.

Becky

Becky came to me as a referral from a friend in Houston. She had just relocated to Austin as a result of a job change for her husband and was settling in to her new city. She had worked as a teacher for two decades in addition to pursuing a burgeoning motivational speaking career in education. With their children grown and gone, Becky decided to take a break from teaching and pursue more speaking opportunities.

With our first meeting limited to introductions and conversation about spiritual direction, Becky was eager to begin when she arrived for our second encounter. We spent most of the appointment getting to know each other, but about forty minutes into our hour-long conversation, there was a pause. As is my custom, I waited for Becky. Tears welled in her eyes as she began again.

"You wouldn't know it by my decisions, but I am miserable every time I have a speaking engagement. Well, actually, I am both miserable and thrilled. This is my calling. This is my gift. I know that. My message to teachers about self-care is so important. What I say is real and wise because I've lived all of it. And it's funny because I am funny," she offered, smiling through the tears. "I know it's effective because people have told me it is. And I'm getting more and more invitations. So why in the world do I feel so horrible *after* the presentation?"

"The tears now are from the horrible feeling?" I asked.

"Some is from that; but it's mostly frustration, and maybe fear. I'm so clueless about why I feel what I feel! There's this big and awful thing inside me that will ruin it all. I have no idea how to figure it out. If I don't figure it out, I know I won't keep going. My dream will die. It's that bad," Becky stated plainly.

"It sounds like self-sabotage, something working in you trying to shut down the good that's happening. That can be a complex and destructive force—we become our own worst enemy," I offered. "Can you say more about the misery? If you close your eyes and take yourself back to that moment, who are you inside? Do you have a different sense of yourself than what people are seeing on the outside?"

She closed her eyes and took a slow, deep breath. After a few moments, she continued, "Definitely. I feel like a little girl cowering in a corner."

"Go on . . . what is she wearing? If she's in a corner, is she in a room? What does it look like? Is anyone else there with her? What is she feeling?" I asked.

"Yes, in a room. She's wearing tattered clothes, like a waif. She's feeling small . . . and shaky. She's thin, small, scared, and hungry. It's so sad," Becky finished.

"Let's stay with the image for a minute, if you can," I invited. "Tell me about the room."

"It's mostly dark. There are big windows on two sides with blinds or heavy curtains. A single shaft of light is coming in so I know it's not dark outside. It's very dusty. It's a library, actually."

"Can you see her face?" I asked.

"Yes. She has a very sensitive, tender face, innocent and sad. She's looking down," she continued.

"Do you know what she is sad about?"

"No," she replied.

"Okay, I think you have a good sense of her. A lot of times, connecting some image of ourselves like you just did with a certain feeling is a good way to be able to talk about that feeling in more concrete terms and to begin to more readily notice when it happens again."

"That was weird. It was so clear when you asked me to imagine who I was." Becky was intrigued.

"Use that image in the next month to be more aware of when you feel that way," I suggested. Our appointment ended shortly thereafter.

When Becky returned a month later, she was excited to report, "I have come up with two times when I felt like that little girl inside. One is from the past and one happened last Sunday," she said excitedly as we began. "For the life of me, I cannot connect them in any way."

"Let's start with the one from last Sunday," I suggested.

"It was in Sunday school. It's a new group for us, just discussion on a Scripture the leader chooses. So about midway through the time, I made a thoughtful comment and the discussion just stopped. The leader said, 'Now that's a profound thought.' " Looking both curious and a little sad she added, "That's when I realized that I felt like that little girl again. I'm not even sure which direction the discussion went after that. I was in my own world of misery."

"I'm sorry for your pain," I said softly.

"Me, too," she said. "The other time was a memory from home. I was seventeen or eighteen and sitting at our kitchen table. Mom was cooking, and I don't remember the subject matter, but I was saying something that was clearly an opinion, not a right or wrong issue. Though she didn't actually move a step from her place at the stove, Mother's words came down on me like this powerful crashing wave that tried to completely obliterate my waif-like self and my waif-like opinion. I couldn't stand at all. I felt like I was drowning, tossed completely upside down like a pebble. It was horrible." Becky took a deep breath. "I think that's the first time I remember feeling like a waif."

"Wow. So in that scene with your mom, the 'waif' was judged to be wrong even when she wasn't wrong . . . so much so that her voice was corrected into oblivion, nonexistence. She was silenced and destroyed. I wonder if you thought your powerful words that silenced the Sunday school class had done some harm. Maybe anything strong feels harmful to you."

"Whoa," she said, "it's not hard to see how that might be sabotaging my public speaking. Can we switch subjects now? I think my brain is about to explode."

Though that conversation was done for the day, over the next many months, Becky and I covered a plethora of topics primarily related to that initial conversation. One of the women we discussed from a parallel story was the wise woman of Abel.

The Wise Woman of Abel

The story of the wise woman of Abel is not an often told tale. Hers is a story of effectual peacemaking in the middle of battle narratives. I find her wisdom to be a hidden treasure, teaching me how courageous feminine initiative can produce real change even in frightening and potentially disastrous situations. For her, that initiative took the form of speaking up; but for others it may well involve actions of a different nature, for example, Rosa Parks sitting on a bus or starting a nonprofit to help a marginalized population. The important dynamic to note and observe is that the wise woman of Abel demonstrates the noble, good, and much-needed soul force of a woman who has effectively avoided self-sabotage and done the holy work of growing up.

Unfolding Disaster

Though our recollections of King David often center on the emotive psalms, he spent most of his life at war, actively battling his numerous enemies. Sheba was a crafty foe of his, referred to as a troublemaker (2 Samuel 20:1). Eventually, Joab, King David's chief military man, caught up with Sheba hiding in the city of Abel and began to attack the city.

Everyone went on with Joab to pursue Sheba son of Bikri.
Sheba passed through all the tribes of Israel to Abel Beth
Maakah and through the entire region of the Bikrites, who

gathered together and followed him. All the troops with Joab came and besieged Sheba in Abel Beth Maakah. They built a siege ramp up to the city, and it stood against the outer fortifications. (2 Samuel 20:13–15)

Taking the Initiative

Clearly, the situation was desperate and not for those faint of heart. When we are young girls, we are protected by others; but when we grow up, we learn that we can take the initiative and enter the battle, not as men, but as wise women of vision. This wise woman had to get very close to the battle to be heard. And make no mistake, she expected to be heard.

While they were battering the wall to bring it down, a wise woman called from the city, "Listen! Listen! Tell Joab to come here so I can speak to him." (2 Samuel 20:15-16)

It is sad to think about how often many women speak without the expectation of being heard. We tell our husbands about our day as they scroll through their BlackBerry email. We tell our children to pick up their socks for the third time. We tell our pastor we are really exhausted while we say yes to another ministry he hands us. We offer new ideas even as we tell everyone why they will never work. We speak up and dismiss ourselves at the same time. We speak without the expectation of being heard, sabotaging and disempowering our own words.

And it's not only with other people. Often we do the same with ourselves, and even with God. Have you ever promised yourself rest and failed to keep your promise? Areas of self-care are the worst: rest, exercise, play, solitude, eating well, personal study, and creativity. Have you promised God that you would pursue some newly inspired and passion-fulfilling endeavor only to renege because you doubt the goodness of your own creative vision?

But this wise woman said, *"Listen! Listen!"* fully expecting to be heard even in the midst of battle. She effectively interjected her strong voice into the fray in an imperative, commanding way. She insisted on speaking to the man in charge.

Going to the Top

He went toward her, and she asked, "Are you Joab?"
"I am," he answered.
She said, "Listen to what your servant has to say."
"I'm listening," he said. (2 Samuel 20:17)

I just *love* this woman's spunk. It is important to keep in mind that she had no idea why this powerful and likely very intimidating-looking man in all his war gear was seeking to destroy her city; yet she demanded to speak to him face-to-face. He could have killed her! She did not seem to flinch as he walked toward her. After verifying that she was indeed speaking to the one in charge, she told him first to listen to her. Interestingly, even as she commanded him to listen, she referred to herself as "your servant." She had a clever way of showing respect and demanding the same from him. She even waited for a response from him before she made her request, verifying that she had his attention.

The way she handled this conversation says to me that she, an unknown, unnamed (for us) woman from Abel, knew that she stood on equal ground with this male military commander. Not above, or below, but beside him. How often we sabotage ourselves, our ideas, our gifts and contributions, and our wisdom by failing to learn and live this simple and critically important truth.

For example, we may talk with our Bible study group about a new idea we have for ministry, but can't quite find the time to make an appointment with the pastor to talk to him about it. Or perhaps we suffer under an abusive immediate supervisor but never mention our pain to her manager. Or we might complain about a lack of recycling in our city but never get around to calling our council representative. Perhaps we refuse to talk to anyone around us at a charity ball because we think *They are out of my league.*

We often take the demure and deferential posture of girlhood in word or in deed, feeling less than. But grounded in a noble understanding of human equality, this wise *woman* went straight to the top and expected to be heard.

Speaking Your Perspective and Questions

She was brief and to the point. She spoke her perspective directly, without waver, hesitation, or apology. She talked about her city both historically and in the present, reframing Joab's actions according to her own vision, and then asking a very well-crafted question.

> She continued, "Long ago they used to say, 'Get your answer at Abel,' and that settled it. We are the peaceful and faithful in Israel. You are trying to destroy a city that is a mother in Israel. Why do you want to swallow up the Lord's inheritance?" (2 Samuel 20:18–19)

Women often speak most powerfully through a descriptive—saying what we see—rather than a prescriptive—telling others what to do—voice. We can cast new vision simply through describing the reality our feminine eyes see. It is often a significantly different reality than is perceived by men.

For several years, I have been trying to find an image that communicates the importance of the church learning to listen to the voices of both women and men and how we all suffer when we hear only one perspective. The best I've come up with thus far is that of our physical vision. God has given us two eyes. Much of what one eye sees the other does also. But there is also a good amount of data that is accessible only to each eye. When the data from both is used cooperatively by our brains, we gain the added dimension of depth perception, which is not possible with either eye on its own.

Sadly, many times women hesitate to share their viewpoint simply *because* it is different. To be fair, we have often experienced rejection by others or even humiliation because of that difference. Yet without our willingness to expect to be respectfully heard as we speak our unique perspective, the whole community suffers.

Effectual, Fruitful Wisdom

"Far be it from me!" Joab replied, "Far be it from me to swallow up or destroy! That is not the case. A man named Sheba son of Bikri, from the hill country of Ephraim, has lifted up his hand against the king, against David. Hand over this one man, and I'll withdraw from the city." (2 Samuel 20:20–21)

Joab clearly heard this courageous woman and seemed genuinely alarmed as he saw his actions through her eyes. It is almost as if her words woke him up to the reality of the impact of his actions, which he likely would never have seen apart from her willingness to boldly interject her voice.

Because of her, he gained a depth of perspective on the situation that changed his strategy altogether. I love the sense in this text that she was able to draw forth from his heart the part of him that genuinely wanted to care for the city at large, to do no more harm than necessary. He explained himself to her and offered her a much better plan. It was *not* a "win-win" proposition with Joab having one agenda and the wise woman a different one. Instead, it was a true unification, with the deeper, larger vision—peace in Israel—achieved.

Wisdom Listens Well

The woman said to Joab, "His head will be thrown to you from the wall." (2 Samuel 20:21)

Though we may cringe at this violent proposal, it is clear that not only men can be fierce. We get a contextual sense of this verse when we look at the way this wise woman described her city: *"a mother in Israel"* (v. 19). Women sometimes joke about becoming fierce mother bears when one of their cubs is in trouble. I think this was one of those moments.

My guess is that our wise woman really listened to Joab—not only to his words but also more intuitively to the sincerity of his concern. She may have known him to be trustworthy by intuition, or perhaps by reputation. When he said this man was dangerous to Israel, she believed him. With limited options within her culture, she knew that sometimes extreme circumstances called for extreme measures. She was open to, received, affirmed, and cooperated with a perspective different than her own.

Two additional observations also intrigue me. First, she was willing to make a quick and decisive choice. Living within our very risk-averse culture, we sometimes fail to see that in certain situations, prudence must include a willingness to be decisive.

Second, she was willing to make an important decision on behalf of her city without consulting anyone else. She possessed a confidence in her knowledge of the people as well as their trust in her. We often hesitate to speak for others, even when we know them well and have evidence of their trust. Often that hesitation is rooted in respect for the other, but sometimes is a result of our own childish insecurity and desire for reassurance.

Advising the Community

Then the woman went to all the people with her wise advice, and they cut off the head of Sheba son of Bikri and threw it to Joab. So he sounded the trumpet, and his men dispersed from the city, each returning to his home. And Joab went back to the king in Jerusalem. (2 Samuel 20:22)

After her face-to-face with Joab, this woman went to *all* the people with her wise advice. Though she had already made a courageous commitment to Joab, she did not act alone in the matter. Though her own word was at risk, she did not command them; she only advised. And they listened. How much courage would it take to know that your words would mean the death of another? My guess is that she did not take any of these choices lightly—but she made them, nonetheless. True to his word, Joab and his men departed.

Giving advice is tricky business. Certainly there are moments when we unwisely inject ourselves into situations for selfish reasons with poor outcomes. Other times, people ask our advice but might not like what they hear and punish us relationally. Though such painful experiences can add important thoughtfulness and temperance to our words, we sometimes overreact and allow them instead to sabotage and silence our voices or actions altogether. Seeking to protect ourselves, we may install accusing, dictating messages like "bossy" or "mind your own business" or "busybody" that silence our wisdom even when our thoughts and actions are actively solicited by others, or we would have good reason to assume our initiative would be welcome and helpful.

Thankfully, this woman of Abel did not give in to self-sabotage. She left the comfort and personal security of girlhood and grew up into a wise woman. Trusted by her people, she was willing to speak, to be heard, to listen, and to make a bold and fierce decision. She risked life and limb, making a friend out of an apparent enemy and powerfully blessing this beloved city she knew as "a mother in Israel."

Becky (continued)

After a year and a half, Becky was in a very different place. Even with a full calendar of speaking engagements, she managed to continue to make our monthly appointments.

"I just loved that poem you gave me last time ["Finding Her Here"]. In fact, I memorized it. I haven't memorized a poem in decades! I *am* finding her here. I'm finding that woman in me that I knew was there . . . the woman who had the passion and the calling and the clarity that her message was a good one."

"And the waif? Is she still with you, too?" I wondered.

"Sometimes. A few weeks ago, in fact, I had a chance to hear a fascinating man speak. He is the newly elected head of the national teachers' association, and his college roommate, Rick, is a friend of mine and the president of our local association. Rick pulled some strings to get him to speak here. I was completely tracking with him philosophically; we are *so* on the same page. It was also pretty clear that not everyone in the room was getting what he was saying.

"After the meeting, I wanted to go up and talk to him, but I didn't. I realized later that evening that the waif dynamic had surfaced and undercut me. That waif in me convinced me that I had nothing of value to add to his big, grown-up world."

Becky took a deep breath. "But I do have something to offer, even to him. I have lots to offer, in fact. Not better, not worse, but good stuff that he doesn't know, especially ways of communicating with teachers. I've got great stories and some really helpful illustrations that teachers still in the classroom really relate to. I taught three times longer than he did and I'm a woman, like the majority of his audience. He really missed out," Becky boldly asserted, then quickly added with a wince and a chuckle, "Is that okay to *say*?"

"Of course it is. He *did* miss out. You both did," I replied. "Self-sabotage is an equal opportunity thief."

"Well, all was not completely lost," Becky said with a smile. "After I realized what had happened, I asked Rick for this man's email address and ended up sending him some of my materials, a few illustrations and such, even a YouTube link. It took him a few weeks, but he emailed me, and we've been going back and forth with this really great conversation! He has been very complimentary."

"Becky, that's wonderful! I'm so glad you didn't give up," I encouraged.

"Wait, wait . . . I'm not finished with the good news: *He* asked *me* for a fee quote yesterday and I'm going up to New York next month to speak to his staff! Isn't that just wild?"

Your *Story*

1. Do you see yourself as wise? Why or why not? How do you feel as you answer?
2. Are there arenas of your life in which you act more like a girl than in others? At home? With your parents? Around men? With peers? At church?
3. On a scale of 1–10 (1 being the least) how seriously do you take your own words? What is your internal response to that number?
4. What is your favorite way of undoing the power of the words you speak to others? Do you fail to hold them accountable for hearing? Do you speak softly or use humor to deflect attention? Do you apologize for speaking? Or offer counterexamples or other reasons, verbal or nonverbal, inviting dismissal of your words? Does your posture change when you speak? If so, how does it change?
5. What is your favorite way to sabotage initiative of other kinds? Do you act impulsively, or wait until your choice is too late to be meaningful? Do you act with unwise independence or resist working through existing authority structures?

6. Who intimidates you? Are there people in whose presence you shut down? With whom would you be afraid or nervous or unable to have a conversation? Why?

7. Has your mothering of something (a child, a cause, a project, someone in your care, yourself) ever moved you to be fierce? Tell the story.

8. How do you feel about the woman of Abel's choice to make such an important decision in the moment? Recall a time when you made an important decision quickly. How did you feel about the outcome? Is there a time when you remained undecided and suffered the loss?

9. When was the last time you made a decision on the behalf of others? For whom are you comfortable making decisions and for whom would you not be comfortable? Why or why not?

13

Choosing to Say Yes to God

Fiat

I uttered myself
I claimed my voice
I was not afraid to question

I held my ground
I made my yes
looking straight into the angel's eyes
(any slave girl could have been beaten or raped
    for less)

There was no mastery here
Nothing was taken from me
Everything was given

Here I am:
See me
    Listen[1]

NICOLA SLEE

CONSIDER: Name three things that you have repeatedly said that you will do someday. Write a book? Take a trip? Plant a garden? Learn a second language? Go back to school? Clean your closet? Train for a marathon? Take a painting class? Start a nonprofit?

Mary P

When I first met Mary, she was in the process of being resurrected by God. We had just moved into a new neighborhood and she happened to be our across-the-street neighbor. Working as the director of evangelism at a local church, she practiced what she preached and invited us to her church, which became ours also. Several months later, I had an opportunity to listen to her story for the first time . . . and what a story it was! This is how I heard it one hot afternoon in May as we sat on her porch and sipped iced tea.

"I guess there's no such thing as a quiet divorce when you are married to a prominent businessman in a small town! It was messy and heartbreaking. I'm sure we all still bear the scars, our children especially. So much pain. And shame. When you grow up as a Southern Baptist from Natchez, Mississippi, divorce isn't even on your radar screen. None of my family understood; shoot, *I* didn't even understand," Mary said with a slight smile and a shake of her head.

"After we divorced, I had to go to work. Boy, was that hard. I'd been really successful in my twenties working for a very upscale hotel in New Orleans. We had moved so much, though, with my husband's job, I had not finished my degree. I had no idea where to begin. Eventually, I landed a job as a recruiter for a local headhunter agency. A few years later, I started a physician's recruiting business of my own. Was that ever a mistake! The economy hiccupped and my business failed, leaving me once again unemployed, now with massive debt to boot." Mary grimaced, evidencing the pain of the memories.

"About that time, I hit such a low that I knew I had to get help. I found a therapist and began two years of weekly, sometimes twice a week, visits. Talk about hard work. Though I thought the divorce and my ex were the primary issues, I quickly discovered that my pain was much more centered on my history of childhood sexual abuse. It felt like this black hole in my soul full of pain that went on forever."

Mary paused. With tears in her eyes, she continued, "I don't know how many times I almost quit. My therapist was so wise. She'd call me on it just before I would throw in the towel." Mary grinned, remembering her counselor. "She'd say something like, 'Mary, after this session, I wouldn't blame you if you wanted to bail on this whole process. But all this work is really getting us somewhere. I know you can't see it yet, but I can. Don't sabotage all the good you have accomplished. Healing happens.' Part of the last work I did with her was to come up with a life mission statement."

"I cannot wait to hear this," I said.

"Here goes: My mission is to bear witness to God's healing and forgiveness, and to be a living monument of God's strength, dignity, and grace," Mary stated with clarity and confidence.

"So is that when you began working for the church?" I inquired, seeking to blend what I was hearing with what I knew of Mary's life now.

"That's another story. I was coming back from a support-group meeting one evening and I realized, all of a sudden really, that I felt a definite call to full-time ministry. Imagine that. Me. Not just a woman, but a *divorced* woman, in the Southern Baptist Church, called to full-time ministry." Mary's face was quite animated as she recalled how ridiculous the thought seemed to her at the time. "Talk about an unlikely candidate!"

She continued, "I didn't do anything with that thought for a long time, but one day, I found myself telling a friend that story. She gave me this really wise advice: 'Mary, you don't have to have it all figured out. Just say yes. The rest is God's job.'

"So I did just that. I said yes. And here I sit today."

I don't think I've ever had a more enjoyable glass of iced tea.

Mary, Mother of Jesus

I used to love to give hurting and frightened patients in the hospital the good news that God has a special place in his heart for rascals. Scripture is replete with tales of shady characters and those whom God used almost in spite of their lack of character. There are, however, some notable exceptions, a few folks who seem to be presented with more perfection than human frailty. One such Old Testament figure is Joseph, the mistreated younger brother turned Pharaoh's chief aide and savior of his people. In the New Testament, we see Mary in the same glowing light, especially in regard to her response to God's calling to become the mother of the Messiah.

An Unexpected Calling

There is a line in one of the closing prayers at church that often stops me in my tracks: "Send us out to do the work you have given us to do."[2] That prayer comes to me at the oddest moments: while clearing seven layers of yard trash after a hurricane, while having a CAT scan of my back, before a spiritual direction appointment. Some of the things God has given me to do in any given week are expected, and some are not. Gabriel's visit to Mary was clearly not an expected event in her life.

In the sixth month of Elizabeth's pregnancy, God sent the angel Gabriel to Nazareth, a town in Galilee, to a virgin pledged to be married to a man named Joseph, a descendant of David. The virgin's name was Mary. The angel went to her and said, "Greetings, you who are highly favored! The Lord is with you."

Mary was greatly troubled at his words and wondered what kind of greeting this might be. But the angel said to her, "Do not be afraid, Mary; you have found favor with God. You will conceive and give birth to a son, and you are to call him Jesus. He will be great and will be called the Son of the Most High. The Lord God will give him the throne of his father David, and he will reign over Jacob's descendants forever; his kingdom will never end." (Luke 1:26–33)

Openness: an easy word to say, a much harder reality to live. Most of us begin life very open, encounter pain along the way (some more, some less), and change our minds. A bit at a time, we close off to the world, shutting out the good as well as the bad. Spontaneity feels problematic; surprises no longer seem fun but threatening.

Perhaps it was youth, perhaps faith, but Mary lived her life with a heart so open toward the new work of God that when Gabriel made his announcement, though "troubled," her only question was "How will this be?"

Faithful Questions Raised

"How will this be," Mary asked the angel, "since I am a virgin?" (Luke 1:34)

It is especially interesting to look at Mary's question as it stands within the text in close proximity to another angelic announcement and questioning response: that of Zechariah. Mary's question evidences her faith and acceptance of the reality that Gabriel had just proclaimed. It was a process question that only makes sense if one assumes that Gabriel was proclaiming truth. It tells us that Mary was not numb or naïve; her brain was engaged and her will already bent toward obedience.

Now look at Zechariah's response just sixteen verses before Mary's. Like Mary, he had been told by Gabriel that he would soon, miraculously, become the parent of a special child.

Zechariah asked the angel, "How can I be sure of this? I am an old man and my wife is well along in years."

The angel said to him, "I am Gabriel. I stand in the presence of God, and I have been sent to speak to you and to tell you this good news. And now you will be silent and not able to speak until the day this happens, because you did not believe my words, which will come true at their appointed time." (Luke 1:18–20)

Rather than a question that assumes the truth of the angelic proclamation, Zechariah doubted the truth and asked for a sign and a guarantee. The only sign he received, being struck mute, feels more like discipline than the guarantee he was seeking.

An Awesome Answer

The angel's answer to Mary's question blows me away. He did not minimize his announcement or seek to make it approachable, contained, or controllable. In no way did he diminish the magnitude of what Mary was considering in order to make her more comfortable. The language he used was immense and intimate, all-consuming.

> *The angel answered, "The Holy Spirit will come on you, and the power of the Most High will overshadow you. So the holy one to be born will be called the Son of God. Even Elizabeth your relative is going to have a child in her old age, and she who was said to be unable to conceive is in her sixth month. For no word from God will ever fail." (Luke 1:35–37)*

So many women spend their lives playing small. I call it ungodly contentment. We find a safe little corner in the world and spend our days maintaining a comfortable nest. Though, of course, such work can be a holy endeavor, it can also be an escape, an unholy refusal to live the life of transformation and faith God is calling us to live. Our penchant for playing small can sabotage our growth and our calling to shine.

Will we, like Mary, consent to the indwelling of the Spirit of God? In powerful and intimate ways? Will we let the greatness of the Most High God come close enough to overshadow our fragile souls, to impregnate us with seeds of inspiration for magnificent, creative, holy, brilliantly shining, and newly born kingdom work? Will we dare to say yes to God?

Interestingly, though Mary did not ask for it, Gabriel gave her a confirming sign: Elizabeth's pregnancy. Note especially that even before she went to verify that transcendent impossibility, she consented to God's invitation without reservation.

No Reservations

"I am the Lord's servant," Mary answered. "May your word to me be fulfilled." Then the angel left her. (Luke 1:38)

I shudder when I stop to take in Mary's words. Blank checks are hard to sign, especially with God. I've often thought, "Okay, God, I give you an inch and you take a mile!" I suppose it is God's to take. I suppose that's why Mary began where she did: "*I am the Lord's servant.*"

Her confession of identity seems significant. She wasn't *doing* something as much as *being* someone. Often as I am seeking God's guidance on what to *do*, the only answer I get is a reminder of *who I am*. As poet Alla Renée Bozarth says, "You will get where you are going by remembering who you are."[3] The obedient life is less about our skill at guessing the right place to put our feet at each moment and more about knowing who we are made to be and offering ourselves to God without reservation, wherever our feet happen to land.

Support Provided, Support Received

God did not ask Mary to walk this path alone: He provided Elizabeth (Luke 1:39–45). Mary enthusiastically received that provision, making what must have been a less than convenient and previously unplanned trip *immediately*.

Women are relational beings all the way down to our intimate biology. When I was living in the dorm at the University of Texas–Austin, I took part in a research project that was investigating how the menstrual cycles of women living in close proximity to one another become synchronized. Mysterious. In yet another demonstration of our biological connection to other women, UCLA published a study several years back that discovered evidence of healing hormones released when women talk about their lives with one another. Such hormones lower both blood pressure and levels of cortisol (a stress hormone that does internal damage to our bodies when elevated). Women need other women, especially during times of stress.[4]

As the social consequences of these impossibilities began to unfold for her, Mary likely needed Elizabeth's comfort and reassurance. She also needed a witness for her celebration.

A Shared Celebration

Rejoice with those who rejoice; mourn with those who mourn. (Romans 12:15)

Both sorrow and joy build tension within our bodies. Larger than our souls can contain, they become experiences that the community is called to share. The splendid spiritual magnitude of the incarnation was not missed by these women. God was doing an altogether new thing, and they were a part of it. Ordinary women with extraordinary callings. No wonder Mary's soul exploded in praise (Luke 1:46–55). Interestingly, Mary's song is largely based on Hannah's song from 1 Samuel 2. Three generations of women who said yes to God were singing the same song of God's goodness and work on behalf of the powerless and lowly, his mercy and salvation. Every time we say yes to God, they sing with us still.

When I witness such large and shared celebrations in Scripture, I am struck by how seldom those kinds of moments happen in many churches today, perhaps due to a misunderstanding of pride. We hesitate to share celebratory news about job promotions, surprising gifts, success, opportunities to shine, awards, or even new insight with one another, fearing that such sharing would be interpreted as bragging or make another person feel bad. Even as I have edited this work, I have squirmed in my seat as I have written wonderful moments experienced with my spiritual direction directees. Me, the woman writing a book on self-sabotage: "I don't want them to think I am showing off. Really, it's God."

Sensitivity to others is good, but when it stifles opportunities for shared celebration and we end up stuffing our joy to the point of damaging our own souls, something has gone wrong.

What a Mess!

Mary's surprising calling wasn't all sweetness and light. There would be challenges: Joseph being the first of many. As we have noted before, women can sabotage or simply refuse to engage any calling from God that will potentially bring pain, suffering, loss, or sacrifice into the lives of those we love. It's one thing for God to ask us to sacrifice; it's altogether another for us to be a part of creating others' loss. Mary had no idea what would happen between her and her fiancé as a result of her consent to her divinely granted calling. For someone completely faithful to God, Mary found herself in quite a predicament.

And poor Joseph had no good options once he found out.

Because Joseph her husband was faithful to the law, and yet did not want to expose her to public disgrace, he had in mind to divorce her quietly. (Matthew 1:19)

What was he to do with Mary's claim of an angelic visit? I am sure he suffered greatly through the decision to put Mary away quietly. Clearly, the text makes a point to tell us that the angel appeared to him in a dream *after* he had considered this. Wouldn't it have been nice if the angel had come to him *before* he knew about the pregnancy? Thank goodness Joseph listened!

There is something in most of us that wants to believe that as long as we are obedient and faithful, God will save us from messy and difficult situations. Such expectations are naïve, certainly not biblical, and a potential setup for self-sabotage. We need to think again. God named his people Israel, which means "one who wrestles with God." Though I don't think God is mean and looking to defeat us, struggle is a part of our lives and therefore a part of our calling, even our calling to shine.

When we refuse that truth and hold on to our perfectionist illusions and life becomes messy anyway, we become distracted by the blame and shame game. Maintaining our belief that messy things only happen to bad people, never to good or responsible people, requires that we define ourselves as bad when our lives become a mess. As we have noted before, it is easier to feel guilty than to wrestle with the painful reality that many times even a godly life is a mess, with no one to blame or shame, with no one at fault.

Surprises Galore: Some Good, Some Bad

First, there were the shepherds. Not the cleaned up version of sheep tenders we might imagine. These guys were smelly, societal lowlifes, disallowed in the temple because they were unclean. Imagine handing your newborn to one of them! I'm not so sure Mary would have considered their visit a good surprise.

But these shepherds told stories of angels. Both Mary and Joseph knew something of angel visits, but not whole choruses of them! Singing! (Luke 2:8–20 THE MESSAGE). Only a few days after the birth, this couple also heard what were likely confusing prophecies as they brought Jesus to the temple for the first time (Luke 2:21–40). Then there were the Magi. They likely arrived later, strange men from a strange land. Again, unexpected company for the little family. These men told quite a tale about a star, and the joy on their faces must have said even more. They worshiped the child and bowed. And the gifts. What a lovely surprise, but what does a poor couple do with such things? (Matthew 2:1–12).

Then there was a surprising and alarming dream and an immediate flight to Egypt (Matthew 2:13–18). This young couple ran for their lives. Reaching home again, likely years later, Mary and Joseph had negotiated all the surprising twists and turns of their new calling successfully. They had not sabotaged this God-ordained adventure by giving up when the surprises were not pleasant. They persevered through highs and lows, great awe and quaking fear. Even still, their life of faith was only beginning.

A Life of New Challenges, a Life of Faith

The child Jesus grew, and with him so did the difficulty. Mary and Joseph spent three anxious days looking for him when he was twelve, only to be told by their son that they should have known where he would be (Luke 2:41–50). Interestingly, for the first time we are clearly told that they did not understand: *"But they did not understand what he was saying to them"* (v. 50). Had it been too long since the angels visited? Their son was no longer a small child; he had a will and had begun to openly identify with God as his Father. Parenting the son of God was not getting any easier. Not to mention the questions that would be raised for Mary in Jesus' ministry and death.

Maybe it's just our American retirement mind-set, but many of us operate with the beloved illusion that life, including our faith journey, will get easier over time. We want to believe that at some point we will begin to coast downhill. If we buy into that illusion, we may cease to hear God's newest invitation and stop asking new, challenging questions, sabotaging our spiritual growth or shining.

Hebrews 11 defines faith in such a way that it requires *not* seeing: *"Now faith is confidence in what we hope for and assurance about what we do not see"* (v. 1). The life of faith is not a journey of decline or coasting. We will always face new challenges. Even death can be seen as the final great leap of faith we will all encounter. No matter how long our journey, our life of faith will always be one in which we are asked to say yes to God as we set out in the dark on the next grand adventure.

Mary P (continued)

I got to know Mary well over the next many years as her neighbor and fellow church member. I also came to know what saying yes to God had cost her. When she left the church of her youth to follow God's call, she experienced genuine loss. Her parents had both been leaders in that tradition and her family did not understand her decision.

Mary's calling took her first into work with a newly formed health clinic for the indigent. A natural networker, she was a pro at gathering resources and organizing them systematically and efficiently, becoming their first program director. After serving there for several years, she accepted the job as director of evangelism at our church only months before I met her, and soon found herself also doing consulting work in the broader church as a congregational coach. Yet even in the midst of her success, Mary's long-standing unfulfilled dream of completing her undergraduate college degree did not go away.

"I know it doesn't seem rational," she began as we talked in my garden one day. "Everyone keeps telling me that my résumé is enough. But I really *want* to go back to school. I love to learn." Her voice was earnest and passionate but dropped quickly; and with a sharp, self-contemptuous tone she added, "Who am I kidding? I am a single mom on a church salary. I'm barely making it as it is. There's just no way this will ever be doable." Yet as much as Mary wanted to kill her pesky dream, it remained at the forefront.

Then came Rita—Hurricane Rita. The storm brought devastation of all kinds: lost jobs, lost homes, lost lives. In the midst of the loss came a huge pause. Wherever one evacuated to, there one remained, for weeks, with little to do but wait and pray, think, and reflect on one's life. When Mary returned, an important shift inside her was well underway. The storm had somehow loosened the soil of her life; the ruts that kept her thinking narrowly focused were disrupted. Mary's soul began investigating a return to school before her mind could argue. Within a few short months, Mary had applied to the school of her choice, been accepted, and was readying her house for the market.

Like her last big leap of faith, this one, also, was not without wonderful surprises and challenging costs. Mary's house did not sell as quickly as she had hoped, so she spent her first semester divided between two cities. At the same time, she found that she loved school more than she had ever imagined possible. She succeeded beyond her own hopes and dreams, continually impressing not only her own professors with her writing and research capabilities, but scholars on a national level, with her papers being published in reputable academic journals! A quick two and a half years later, I watched her long-held dream come true as she graduated with highest honors.

"So what's next, Mary?" I asked over coffee not long after graduation.

"I'm not sure yet." Mary laughed deeply with a twinkle in her eye, "But as Helen Keller said, 'Life is either a daring adventure or nothing!' Here's to the next grand adventure!"

Your Story

1. If time, money, and energy resources were not an issue, list five things you would do. Reflecting on your own story, can you tell where the seed of each desire is sourced?

*The place God calls you to is the place where your
deep gladness and the world's deep hunger meet.*[5]

FREDERICK BUECHNER

2. Name as many points of "deep gladness" as you can. These are moments when all of who you are is fully engaged in some endeavor, you are utterly joyful to your core, and the results are satisfyingly fruitful. Nothing is too large or too small to mention.

3. Where do you most see "the world's deep hunger"? Sometimes you can tell by what really makes you angry or upset.

4. When are you most likely to play small? Describe the last incident.

5. Have you ever said yes to God and found yourself in a messy life situation? Tell the story.

6. What do you most admire about Mary? Joseph? What about your own faith journey?

7. In your life of faith, where are you walking by faith, setting out in the dark, without seeing?

8. Recall your most exciting faith adventure. Tell the story this week.

9. Have you ever said no to God? What did you gain? What was the cost?

10. Is there a new grand adventure invitation before you now?

Conclusion

I'm Gonna Let It Shine

I confess: Sometimes I get bored in church. When I do, my mind often wanders to the stories of women in Scripture. Not long ago, I did that very thing and found myself thumbing through the Gospels looking for one of the Martha and Mary stories to answer a question that had popped into my head. Before I located what I thought I was looking for, I stumbled across the story of Jesus' Sabbath day healing of the bent-over woman.

I have been writing about the stories of women in Scripture for years, but somehow I had missed this one. Though I'm sure I'd read it before, in this particular reading of the story I began to see it as iconic, as a story that introduced me to an image (standing tall) that gathered within its experience so many of the other stories we have studied in this book.

Though I have minimal formal training as a writer, I know enough not to mix my metaphors, especially this late in the book. We have been talking all along about our calling to shine, not our calling to stand tall. But as I ventured down this path of thought, I began to see it not as a mixing of metaphors, but as a completion of the picture, as a fuller image of our feminine calling to shine. Here's what I read and discovered that day.

> *On a Sabbath Jesus was teaching in one of the synagogues, and a woman was there who had been crippled by a spirit for eighteen years. She was bent over and could not straighten up at all. When Jesus saw her, he called her forward and said to her, "Woman, you are set free from your infirmity." Then he put his hands on her, and immediately she straightened up and praised God.*
>
> *Indignant because Jesus had healed on the Sabbath, the synagogue leader said to the people, "There are six days for work. So come and be healed on those days, not on the Sabbath."*
>
> *The Lord answered him, "You hypocrites! Doesn't each of you on the Sabbath untie your ox or donkey from the stall and lead it out to give it water? Then should not this woman, a daughter of Abraham, whom Satan has kept bound for eighteen long years, be set free on the Sabbath day from what bound her?"*
>
> *When he said this, all his opponents were humiliated, but the people were delighted with all the wonderful things he was doing. (Luke 13:10–17)*

Many Women Live Bent Over, Crippled by a Spirit

This book has been written over a two-year, self-imposed sabbatical that I took after working seven years as a hospital chaplain. As this manuscript and that allotted time began to move toward an end, I found myself prayerfully pondering, "What next?" Alongside that question, I was also studying

Ephesians with a small group at church. As I listened, God used those Scriptures to affirm my calling to minister to women. Like Paul, I feel a stewardship of a message. His was preaching the gospel to the Gentiles. Mine is helping women see the healing and affirming love of God for their feminine souls through the stories of women in Scripture. Even as I write this, I feel myself standing taller.

But that's not the whole story. As I read this story in church that day, I was immediately aware of a huge "bent over posture" arena in my life: marketing. How many times have I said, "I'm an introvert; I'm no good at marketing"? Though I believe deeply in these healing messages, I cringe and bend when I think of actually making a cold call and sharing the messages with other people. The *Just who do you think you are?* rant begins anew. Here I am, a woman who has written an entire book on self-sabotage, bent over, hiding my light, struggling against myself as my own worst enemy.

My continual temptation in marketing is to regress to my girlish self and beg and plead for God to send some knight in shining armor to save me. God also challenged me on that one this summer. Paul's prayer for the Ephesians was for God to strengthen them through his Spirit in their "inner being" (3:16). The consistency of this message was becoming utterly annoying! Will I ever dare to answer the rant and boldly say, "I am a woman called by God with a stewardship of a healing and freeing message for women!"?

As if to underline my need to stand tall, the same month I read that story, I began a new treatment approach for a very old problem of sciatica in my right leg. You guessed it: A significant part of the approach had to do with standing and sitting very tall to maintain the arch in my back. When I would slump, the pain would begin in my leg. When I stood tall, it would leave. Okay, okay! I get the message. The reason this story struck me so profoundly that day is because I *am* the woman crippled by a spirit and bent over. Once more, I need Jesus' healing touch.

For generations, many women have faulted forces outside of themselves, such as patriarchy and faulty societal and church structures as the cause of their bent-over status. Certainly such injustice was and at times is real and does real harm. It has often been the voice that has first given us the shaming *Just who do you think you are?* accusation. Yet in the midst of living with more freedom than women have ever known, we still struggle. Often without knowing it, we adopt those accusing words as our own and say them over and over to ourselves. This bent-over posture is as much about our individually crippled spirits and lives as it is about the collective flaws in society or the church.

As we look at the gathered messages of these stories of women, this bent-over posture is a theme woven through many of the lives we have encountered. Think of Lot's wife bent over with a limited imagination and vision. Remember the woman caught in adultery, bent over in shame, waiting for the stones to fall. Or Martha, bent over with a heart full of resentment toward her sister, feeling unloved by Jesus, and only seeing herself as a servant rather than a beloved friend. Recall the cynicism and walls raised by the woman at the well that kept her tender, hurting heart carefully hidden beneath a tough exterior. We also looked at Hannah, whose enormous pain weighed her spirit low until "Hannah stood up." Think once more about the woman with the hemorrhage who, quite literally, was bent low when she reached out in faith and touched the hem of Jesus' garment.

Jesus Saw Her

Note that the woman bent over had not come to Jesus asking for healing. Instead, he saw her and offered it. So often, we do not even notice our bent posture. I had suffered beneath the load of accusing voices within for years (actually *decades*) before I became aware of them. Often we don't know anything else. Our bending has overtaken us slowly, like the frog that doesn't recognize its need to leap from the gradually boiling water. Forces within and without our souls have worked in concert to weigh us down. Our mothers and grandmothers may well never have questioned their own posture of limitations. So why do we question them now?

The stories we have traversed in this book speak a loud message that God greatly values the gifts, voices, and personhood of women. If we will dare to simply see and take seriously all that God has written into these texts, we will no longer be content to live as women crippled by a spirit and bent over. We will begin to answer the rant with words like "I am a woman who has been touched by God and freed to stand tall."

Jesus Called Her Forward

The consistent direction of growth for women in these stories is toward a larger sense of personhood and a greater sense of voice. This message runs so counter to what we have been taught. Yet time and time again we have seen God affirming and elevating and shining a brilliant light on women who stand tall.

Think of Tamar, who stood tall and battled injustice with cunning, being declared "more righteous" in the end.

Remember the wise woman of Abel, who stood toe-to-toe with Joab, winning safety for her people. Or Naomi, who took on God himself in her bitterness of soul and was given new life through a grandson. Alongside her, we have read about the Syrophoenician woman who stood tall through her unapologetic and unpretentious request as she begged for the healing of her daughter, which Jesus in turn credited to her gutsy response.

Certainly Scripture affirms Queen Esther's courage and skill as a leader and savior of her people. Also recall the visionary and creative Mary of Bethany, who bravely anointed Jesus in the midst of a critical crowd. And we cannot forget Mary the mother of Jesus, who stood tall and welcomed the very presence of the Lord God Almighty into her body and soul as she said yes to God. Through each of these stories, recorded so long ago for our sake and for wisdom, God is still calling women forward into vital relationship with him, powerful presence and voice in the world.

Jesus Did Not Fix Her, He Freed Her

It may sound like insignificant semantics, but bear with me. A huge part of our bent-over posture as women comes from a false understanding of ourselves as hopelessly flawed and therefore unlovable as we are. The good news of Jesus offers us a radically different message: God loved and loves us in the midst of our flaws. He sent Jesus while we were still sinners. In Christ, nothing can separate us from the love of God.

When God sees us bent over, God does not respond, "Shame on her; she should know better. What good can she do me in that posture? Let me fix that problem." Though, I confess, that is how I took the message of this story at first. Perhaps you have read this whole book in that way.

When I looked more closely, I saw that this story is not about correcting bad behavior but about a deep compassion that initiates and an abundant freedom that heals and empowers. Jesus did not fix her, he *freed* her. Jesus did not approach her as a taskmaster, wanting to make his servant more effective and efficient. He approached her as a lover, hurting for her and envisioning beautiful possibilities. He initiated the healing, calling her forward and touching her to make a dream she had never dared envision a living reality.

Some Objected, Jesus Defended

For whatever reason, some people become very angry in the presence of a woman who has been freed to stand tall. The synagogue rulers, possessing more compassion for their oxen than for this woman, objected to her healing on the Sabbath. Jesus compassionately highlighted her suffering and exposed their hard hearts, defending his decision to free her without delay. He would not tolerate another minute of bondage. What a holy impatience!

Once again, this iconic story gives voice to a common theme: objection and defense. When Mary stood tall by sitting at Jesus' feet to learn, Martha had a fit! Jesus not only defended Mary, he also invited Martha to see that she, too, could be freed from her bent posture of living as one "worried and bothered." When Mary stood tall and anointed Jesus, Judas objected. Jesus defended her again. When Jesus stopped to wait for the woman with the hemorrhage to speak up, his disciples thought he was crazy. They also wondered at his willingness to talk with the Samaritan woman at the well.

When we face resistance, may we hear Jesus' voice over the voice of our critics.

Many Celebrated

In this story of healing "the people were delighted." The freeing of women to stand tall and shine is a part of the "wonderful things" God is doing in the world, both then and now. It is not a women's issue alone; it is a church issue. It is a part of the collective witness of Christ's body. Many believed because of the testimony of the woman at the well. She was a woman who learned not to be invisible but to stand tall and embrace an intimate relationship with her Messiah. This is kingdom work for all of us.

As we have journeyed together, my sincere prayer has been that through these profound stories and simple words you will have experienced the lavish love of God for your feminine soul in new and deeper ways. I pray that together we will have come to know and begun to listen to the shining wisdom of these wise women that can silence the destructive voice of self-sabotage. I also pray that God's love and their wisdom may give you a clear and firm response when *Just who do you think you are?* echoes in your head. Changing the world and the church begins in the small moments when we refuse to become our own worst enemy. We will not tolerate another minute of bent-over bondage! May we, like Jesus, live with a new and holy impatience. May each of us, in freedom and grace, stand tall and shine like never before!

My response is to get down on my knees before the Father, this magnificent Father who parcels out all heaven and earth. I ask him to strengthen you by his Spirit—not a brute strength but a glorious inner strength—that Christ will live in you as you open the door and invite him in. And I ask him that with both feet planted firmly on love, you'll be able to take in with all followers of Jesus the extravagant dimensions of Christ's love. Reach out and experience the breadth! Test its length! Plumb the depths! Rise to the heights! Live full lives, full in the fullness of God.

God can do anything, you know—far more than you could ever imagine or guess or request in your wildest dreams! He does it not by pushing us around but by working within us, his Spirit deeply and gently within us.

> *Glory to God in the church!*
> *Glory to God in the Messiah, in Jesus!*
> *Glory down all the generations!*
> *Glory through all millennia! Oh, yes!*
>   (Ephesians 3:14–21 THE MESSAGE)

Notes

Introduction This Little Light of Mine

1. Irenaeus, *Adversus Haereses,* Book IV, chap. 20, no. 7.

Chapter One The Unimagined Life

1. Rainer Maria Rilke, "Herr: Wir sind armer den die armen Tiere," in *Rilke's Book of Hours: Love Poems to God,* translated by Anita Barrows and Joanna Macy (New York: Riverhead Books, 1996), 95. Used by permission of Riverhead Books, an imprint of Penguin Group (U.S.A.), Inc.

2. Brian Taylor, *Becoming Human* (Cambridge, MA: Cowley, 2005), 207.

3. *Chariots of Fire,* directed by Hugh Hudson (1981; Warner Home Video, 2005), DVD.

Chapter Two The Unworthy Life

1. Brene Brown, *The Gifts of Imperfection* (Center City, MN: Hazelden, 2010), 23.

Chapter Three The Unlived Life

1. Edwina Gateley, "The Dying," in *Psalms of a Laywoman* (Franklin, WI: Sheed & Ward, 1999), 42–43. Used with permission. Sheed & Ward is an imprint of Rowman and Littlefield Publishers, Inc.

Chapter Five Creativity: Conformity vs. Uniqueness

1. Alla Renée Bozarth, "What Is Prayer?" in *Moving to the Edge of the World* (Lincoln, NE: iUniverse, 2001), 311. All rights reserved. For more information or permission to reprint, contact the poet by email: allabearheart@yahoo.com.

Chapter Six Shining: Recoiling vs. Radiance

1. Mary Anne Radmacher, "The Jump Is So Frightening" poster, www.maryanneradmacher.com/cgi-bin/plugins/MivaEmpresas/miva?plugins/MivaMerchants/merchant.mvc+Screen=PROD&Store_Code=WG&Product_Code=01007&Category_Code=Z5-FAVP. Used with permission. maryanneradmacher.net.

Chapter Seven Choosing Vulnerability

1. Hafiz, "Your Mother and My Mother," in *The Gift: Poems by Hafiz the Great Sufi Master,* translated by Daniel Ladinsky (New York: Penguin Compass, 1999), 39. Used by permission.

Chapter Eight Choosing to Say No

1. Alla Renée Bozarth, "Women's Confession," in *Accidental Wisdom* (Lincoln, NE: iUniverse Publishers, 2003), 171. All rights reserved. For more information or permission to reprint, contact the poet by email: allabearheart@yahoo.com.

Chapter Nine Choosing to Tell Your Story

1. Bernice Johnson Reagon, "Bernice Johnson Reagon in Conversation on October 22, 2003," *Smithsonian Folkways,* www.folkways.si.edu/explore_folkways/bernice_reagon.aspx.

Chapter Ten Choosing to Re-Create in the Midst of Loss

1. Edwina Gateley, "Letting Go," in *Psalms of a Laywoman* (Franklin, WI: Sheed & Ward, 1999), 110–111. Used with permission. Sheed & Ward is an imprint of Rowman and Littlefield Publishers, Inc.

Chapter Eleven Choosing to Persevere in the Midst of Injustice

1. International Commission of English in the Liturgy, "Psalm 137," in *The Canticles: A Faithful and Inclusive Rendering from the Hebrew and Greek into Contemporary English Poetry, Intended Primarily for Communal Song and Recitation.* (Chicago: Liturgy Training Publications, 1996).

Chapter Twelve Choosing to Grow Up

1. Jayne Relaford Brown, "Finding Her Here," in *I Am Becoming the Woman I've Wanted,* edited by Sandra Haldeman Martz (Watsonville, CA: Papier-Mache Press, 1994), 1.

Chapter Thirteen Choosing to Say Yes to God

1. Nicola Slee, "Fiat," in *The Book of Mary* (Harrisburg, PA: Morehouse Publishing, 2007), 19. Used by permission. All rights reserved.

2. *The Book of Common Prayer*, www.bcponline.org/HE/he2.htm, 366.

3. Bozarth, "Passover Remembered," in *Womanpriest: A Personal Odyssey* (Philadelphia: Innisfree Press, 1988). All rights reserved. For more information or permission to reprint, contact the poet by email: allabearheart@yahoo.com.

4. Gale Berkowitz, "UCLA Study on Friendship Among Women: An alternative to fight or flight," in *Psychology Review,* July 2000.

5. Frederick Buechner, *Wishful Thinking: A Theological ABC* (New York: Harper Collins, 1993), 119.

JANET DAVIS has a master's degree in spiritual nurture (Western Seminary–Seattle) and works as a spiritual director, writer, and speaker after many years in hospital chaplaincy. She has published two books: *The Feminine Soul: Surprising Ways the Bible Speaks to Women* and *Sacred Healing: MRIs, Marigolds, and Miracles*. Janet and Bob, her husband of more than thirty years, live in Austin, Texas. She enjoys their four adult children, gardening, and good food.